The Routes of English

by
Simon Elmes

BBC RADIO 4

Foreword by Melvyn Bragg

Spoken English drives the language and this series, **The Routes of English**, goes down that road. Written English has nailed and enhanced spoken English time and again, but the tongue has always had its say. In shade of expression and idiosyncratic precision, the spoken word can often out-fox the scripted version – as I know from local experience with the Wigton dialect in Cumbria. It may be lost to the national stock of words but is full of depth and charge to those few in the know.

This series uses many of the techniques of radio to provide a word picture of our words. Linguistic experts have contributed to it, but it is not solely or even largely an academic exercise. There are street interviews, historical references, discussions – it is not comprehensive but it is, I believe, full of the flavour and the love of our language sweeping through the last one thousand years.

The wealth of English Literature (and it is about English, not Gaelic, Welsh, Cornish or even Cumbrian) is tapped only when it provides contemporary evidence about the spoken word. When the authors are Chaucer and Shakespeare there is good reason to trust their ears.

In one way we have made it difficult for ourselves because the outer limit of our recordings of actual spoken English is about 150 years. But medieval texts were written to be spoken aloud. Communal story telling was the way even kings were educated. William I could neither read nor write and illiteracy predominated until two or, at the most, three centuries ago.

Why a thousand years? Well, the Millennium bug is catching. And about a thousand years ago there appeared the first document of English taking the form of a conversation – Ælfric's *Colloquy*. The story we tell is anchored in different parts of the country. It could start anywhere – but Simon Elmes, the producer, decided to begin in my old home town of Wigton in north Cumbria. There, as everywhere, we discovered a rich mix – including in Wigton, Norse and Romany – which over the centuries was stirred into sounds and words which now enrich and encircle the globe.

Introduction by Simon Elmes

To speak...talk...converse...chat ...discuss...communicate. Spoken language is so different from the written word, from these words you are reading now. It is where sounds change, where new words are often first coined – perhaps by accident – and where grammar gets distorted or modified. Spoken English has been likened to a slowly moving glacier which changes as it goes, introducing new ways of describing our world as new things are made, new concepts imagined, new fashions whipped up.

This book and two CDs which accompany the BBC Radio 4 series, The Routes of English, are about **spoken** English in the UK, as are the radio programmes. They are based on the transcripts and interviews gathered for the series. We take listeners and readers on a journey through a thousand years of talking in the English tongue. We visit six key locations along this linguistic road and explore some of the landmark moments, as well as the great thematic connections that join our 'now' to a historical 'then'.

And language, too, is power. From the earliest times, those who have a command of the language which is used for government and is spoken by the leaders of a community, state or nation will be in the best position to negotiate or persuade. They will have access to power and therefore wealth. The language of influence changes for

St Augustine brings Christianity and literacy to England	Approximate date of the Anglo-Saxon poem 'Beowulf'	Viking raids begin	Alfred becomes King of Wessex	Danelaw boundaries settled – confining the Danes to East of England	Norman Conquest	Chaucer's main works, such as the Canterbury Tales written	Wyclif's translation of the Bible into English	The Great Vowel Shift – bringing a change into the sound of spoken English	C i t p E

different reasons. A country may be invaded as England was by the Danes, or it ma
be conquered as it was by the Normans. New languages may come in as a result o
trade with other countries or because immigrants arrive, seeking refuge for political
financial or religious reasons. They bring their own vocabulary with them, some o
which creeps gradually into the host language.

The journey along these routes of the spoken English language begins at home. I
Melvyn Bragg's home town, in fact: Wigton in Cumbria. How, he asks, have
Wigtonians spoken about their home-turf across the thousand years of the second
millennium? In the eleventh century, unless you were highly educated – which
probably meant that you were a priest or a scholar or both – you could neither write
words, nor read them – so you spoke them. The world was full of talk, though that talk
was very local.

In Chapter Two, Melvyn takes his expert witnesses, featuring some of Britain's most
engaging academic authorities, to the medieval city of Winchester in Hampshire
where King Alfred had his Court and which was at the heart of the local variety o
English which gained precedence in the year 1000. But how local is the talk o
Winchester today?

From Winchester, the route heads down to Hastings in Sussex to examine the ways

508	1549	1603	1623	1707	1755	1800–1910	1884–1928	1922	1940–1975
nting roduced in tland	Book of Common Prayer written	English and Scottish monarchies united under James I	First Folio of Shakespeare's plays published	Treaty of Union between England and Scotland	Samuel Johnson's 'Dictionary of the English Language'	Main period of Irish and European emigration to England and America	Compilation of the Oxford English Dictionary	British Broadcasting Corporation set up	Main period of immigration to Britain from the Caribbean and Asia

the language of France has shaped English since their first successful incursion in 1066. Canterbury is the next destination of our linguistic travellers, as it was of the pilgrims in Geoffrey Chaucer's great medieval account in verse of the world of the late fourteenth century, *The Canterbury Tales*. Chaucer's English and that of the citizens of medieval Canterbury was called Middle English. Less than a hundred years later, with the arrival of printing and the ability more easily to 'fix' and standardise the slippery shapes of the spoken tongue, English was recognisably modern, as we learn in Chapter Five. Now English is shipping vast freights of new words to describe the expanding known world where great powers vie for supremacy; this takes the book to Edinburgh a place symbolic of the struggle between the English and Scots language, a struggle inextricably bound up with the political debate which still goes on today.

Finally Liverpool, perched on the very edge of England, both reflects all these facets of language and seems to give them a new direction. For centuries it has looked outwards to the New World, first for trade and secondly as a gateway to a new life for millions of people, not only from Britain and Ireland, but from all over Europe. It has given hope to those passing through and provided a refuge for those that stayed, enriching itself by this vibrant clatter of cultures. Here is a snapshot of a truly multilingual city.

contents

W

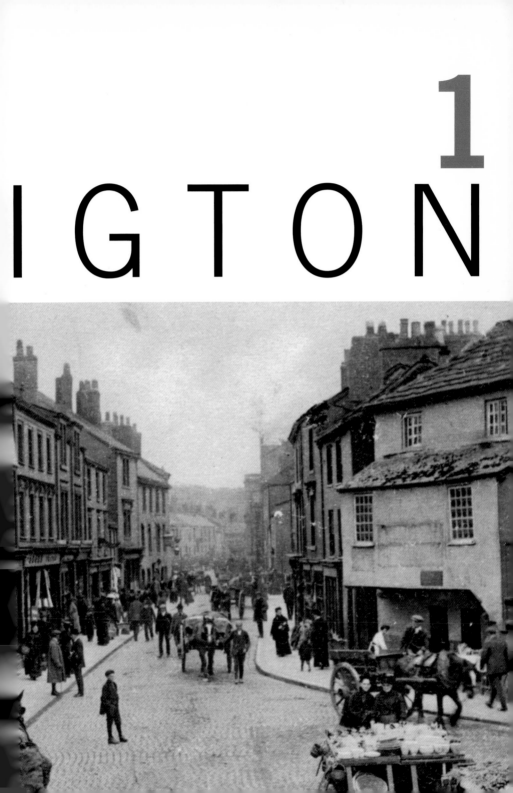

Wigton is a working town. It breathes industry and industriousness. And yet it is still a country place, surrounded by farmland, in that tucked away corner of Cumbria that neither belongs to Carlisle and the North, nor has much in common with the big boned country of the Lake District to the south. The town, which has only about five thousand inhabitants and is barely more than a big village, is clustered around a busy main street and snagged crossroads, with a sandstone church standing a little apart from today's main thoroughfare.

There is a sense of Wigton being caught in time. The shops seem to belong to an older age. George Johnson's, the shoe-shop with its counter wall a pigeon loft of boxes, looks scarcely at home with today's Doc Martens and latest Kickers. William Ismay's café rattles with the clatter of pots and chunky china, while customers drift out to the little travelling fair – just a couple of roundabouts and straggly stalls set up on a patch of open ground across the way. Cars surge past the knots of youths hanging about waiting for something to happen.

Down the hill is The Factory. Melvyn Bragg's own father worked here once, as have done generations of Wigtonians. The Factory is the town's lifeblood – one thousand or so men and women earn their living there, which means that, if the business goes under, so does Wigton. Nowadays, it is a state-of-the-art plastics outfit making, amongst other things, the transparent film that wraps up cigarette packets. Its business horizons lie well beyond the fells of Cumbria, with subsidiaries in Australia, the U.S. and Germany. Yet, on the factory floor, the accents are still as broad as on the farms that in Melvyn Bragg's childhood used to extend almost into the heart of the town.

Wigton was, and still is, home to Melvyn Bragg. It may be short on touristic temptations

14

but is a place which nonetheless thrives in his imagination. He reads the streets like a gazetteer, remembering with what he calls 'this almost burdensome total recall' the people who lived there and special places that still echo with the voices of the boys he played *chessy* with, as they chased down the narrow back-alleys and across the roofs of this playground of his childhood.

Where better, then, than here to explore the notion of 'home' and the words we have used to describe it, across one thousand years of history in these islands. For if there are few obvious delights for the non-specialist eye in Wigton, the ear is by contrast richly served. This is an accent that crackles and gargles in the mouths of Wigtonians. Vowels are tugged as far as they can stretch from 'Received Pronunciation' English and consonants breathed into different shapes to mislead the ignorant outsider.

Then there are the words. There are strange sounding imports from tinker's talk, or cant, like *ducal* for dog, *chava* for child and *gadji* for man. They are Norse words, woven in a thousand years ago, and now so deep in daily talk that they barely sound out of place, yet words like *yet* for gate, *yam* for home and *yak* for oak give Wigton conversation a whiff of the fjords.

Melvyn Bragg described his feelings for his home town:

I come home to Wigton perhaps ten or twelve times a year, and there is a sense in which I scarcely feel I've left it. Whenever I come back, I'm just absolutely rivetted by the place: what's the same, what's changed, who lives where. I'm infatuated by it, I suppose. I physically left when I was eighteen, to go to university, but have been coming back regularly ever since. I don't quite know why, but I get really excited every time I come to Wigton. It's to do with   almost just exploring the streets, the shops, the names, the people I see, the back-

alleys I used to play in.

Looking up Market Hill, I can remember fun fairs there just after the war, and the pub, the 'Blackie' – the Blackamoor Hotel so-called – where I went when I was aged eight. Then there's the grammar school which is now a house, and behind it, there's a high walled garden which I used to break into from the back of the Blackamoor – across the roof of the lavatories on to the wall – to raid the orchard in there. Where there's a gap in one of these alleys we used to go through what was called 'Toppins Field'. It was a proper farm field right in the middle of the town, where we'd go and play football. Actually, what we did really, was what we used to call to get *chessed*. There was a quite bad tempered fellow living up there and, if you taunted him enough, he would chase – *chess* – you; and that was great because you could always run faster than him, and lose him down in the back alleys of the bottom lanes.

The place just intoxicates me all the time. It was a curious time through the war and just after the war there seemed to be everything that anybody could want in Wigton – a lot of youth clubs, all sorts of people. There was a gypsy camp, too, and there were the fair people. We

This carnival picture shows a national event being acted out locally in Wigton by one family. Father, brother and son recreate the 1923 Derby with the owner, trainer and jockey, and, of course, the horse.

spoke a language which was very particular to this town. It was a thick Cumbrian dialect, full of Viking words, *ower yonder, yet, yak, yam,* that sort of thing. It had Romany words, it had Norse words, it had Indian words... And people liked to speak broad.

'Broad' they have always spoken in Wigton. But in the eleventh century all varieties of English were to a large extent 'broad' because the words you used and the sound they made depended on where you lived. It was, though, essentially, Old English.

Dr Kathryn Lowe of the University of Glasgow, who has worked closely with Melvyn Bragg in the making of The Routes of English, makes the point that essentially the language we speak today is very heavily derived from that same Old English or, as it is sometimes called, Anglo-Saxon:

Virtually all the everyday nouns we use – 'earth', 'stone', 'sheep', 'cow'; the vocabulary of familial relationship – 'brother', 'sister', 'father' – are all Old English. And we've hung onto that native stock. Some words have shifted their meaning, but very few have been lost. However, in medieval times, regional varieties often showed huge differences from each other, such that a person living in Cumbria, say in the year 1000, who bumped into a Londoner would have thought they spoke very strangely indeed. In fact, each would have used many words which were completely incomprehensible to the other. For example, even a word like 'good' would have been pronounced markedly differently from the south to the north of Britain. It is not, of course, the case that, if one were standing half way down the country, people on one side would be saying one type of vowel and on the other side they would be saying it another way, but it's a continuous shading. Even today, if you take a long train journey and you get off several times, you'll hear the accents change. If you've got a lot of closely-spaced stations, you'll only hear the accents changing a little bit.

In another conversation Melvyn Bragg asked **Professor Katie Wales** from Leeds

University about the north-south divide:

Northumbrian English was certainly quite strikingly different from West Saxon and Kentish English, as it is today. Midlands or Mercian English was neither one thing nor another. Culturally speaking the North had been one of the first of the Anglo Saxon kingdoms to be civilised. There had been great centres of learning at Jarrow, Lindisfarne and Wearmouth, but by the eleventh century the prestige had moved southwards to Winchester, not London. Actually I think that King Alfred in the ninth century was responsible for one very distinctive north-south divide politically speaking, when he made a truce in the late 870s with the Vikings and said, well, it's okay you can settle north of this line. That's the Danelaw which runs from the Mersey diagonally across to the Thames Estuary, so I think there was very much a sense of a north-south divide and in fact the place name, Northumberland, means precisely that in the Anglo-Saxon period. Northumberland covered the North-West as well as the North-East and it meant, literally, 'lands north of the Humber' so the Humber divided north from south.

In Cumbria, though, the northern variety of Old English that was spoken at the end of the first millennium was subject to influences that in many ways made it quite different from southern Englishes, and above all from the Old English standard. 'Standard' English at the time was essentially a written standard, a literary standard, based in Winchester. However, the essential position throughout the Middle Ages was really that everybody spoke their own variety. If they wanted a standard the educated people spoke Latin.

The north-west of Britain is a very good place to start to survey the history of the language because it is so distinctive. An eleventh-century Wigtonian would have spoken Old English spiked with a strong flavour of Old Norwegian or Old Icelandic, because of the Viking and

Norwegian settlements that had been set up in the North-West since the ninth century. It would also have sounded very much like what is now thought of as northern or lowland Scottish. By the end of the tenth century, there was a distinct northern dialect, as documents and the explanatory footnotes on them reveal, as well as in place names. So there would have been a very distinctive kind of speech spoken in Wigton, with a particularly interesting set of vowels that were very much influenced by the Viking (especially Norwegian) settlement, and it's a local speech form that is still very strong in rural Cumberland today.

Melvyn Bragg asked **Professor Wales** about the position of eleventh century Cumbria in the dialect map of the United Kingdom. She explained that Wigton can be seen as the focus for a wide range of different speech forms, stemming from its position within the ancient territory of Cumberland. The north-west of England can be shown to reveal several other varieties of north-south divide beyond the simple one as drawn by the Danelaw. For example, you could place a town like Wigton, linguistically speaking, in relation to the villages that lie directly round about it (something you can still do today), then you can place the county of Cumberland within what's sometimes called by dialectologists the 'six northern counties' – in relation to Westmoreland to the south, and to the Scottish border northwards. In some cases there are strong resemblances between Cumberland and Northumberland just over the top across the Pennines. Cumberland talk can be compared to the speech of 'the far north' versus the 'lower north' (Yorkshire

This photograph comes from Wilkinson's Photographers in Wigton, who displayed in their windows photos o' local events. At a time when individuals did not have their own cameras, people could buy the scenes they fancied.

Here a *york* is crossing a flooded *beck*. A *york* is ar older northern word for any wagon and horse (th southern word being *drey*.) A *beck* is a northern wor for a minor rive

is thought of, in this context, as being the 'lower north'), and to parts of Lancashire. So you've got these very small dialect areas spreading out to larger dialect areas. Wigton, therefore, could be the focus of quite a number of dialect variables. **Professor Wales** also talked about examples of expressions at the heart of the Wigton dialect:

You find vocabulary and proverbial expressions in the rural speech of Cumberland which you don't find in any other places. For example, I noticed recently that if somebody wanted to ask the way in Cumberland a farmer might say well he's going to *spere* the road and *spere* comes straight from the Old English verb *speriam* meaning to ask. Some flower and plant names are peculiar to Cumberland and proverbial expressions like '*daft as a yet that opens baith ways*' meaning 'daft as a gate that opens both ways' or '*daft as a swill*' meaning 'daft as a basket'. These are very localised expressions. Clearly the vocabulary isn't the same as it was a hundred years ago, or even in your (Melvyn Bragg's) day., The children in Cumberland don't go to work in the fields or on the farms. They are educated at school now, so the vocabulary related to farming, and also to some extent fishing, will inevitably disappear. However, dialect isn't only words and it isn't only grammar, of course. It's a distinctive way of speaking. Young people have a very distinctive accent and there is a lot of talk about the spread of glottal stops from estuary English in London. If people want to sound northern, if they want their own identity and to preserve their regional identity, they will do that. By young people, particularly, it's often seen as a sign of 'macho-ness' or solidarity to preserve your local accent.

The Romans occupied the area for seven hundred years and, a mile from the centre of Wigton, they established a huge and important camp, housing a thousand cavalry patrolling a huge tract of territory against marauders, especially Celts. Yet there is no significant linguistic trace from Latin or from the Roman era. This is explained by the fact that, after 410 when the

Romans withdrew from the land, it is the Celtic influence that reasserted itself.

Melvyn Bragg then discussed with **William Rollinson** of Liverpool University and author of *The Cumbrian Dictionary*, the successive waves of linguistic influence and the traces that have been left on the way Wigtonians speak today:

The Celts left their mark on the speech of Cumbria, and today this is clearly visible in certain

Gypsy families used to be familiar visitors to Wigton when horse fairs, held locally, were important annual events. They camped in the village on High Moor for several days with their horses and brought a different culture and language with them. Many Romany words became part of the local dialect. The Romany word for a horse was *grey*, meaning not just a white horse, but any horse. Locals still talk of a good horse being a *good grey*.

place names: 'P*en*', '*Tor*', '*Blen*' – names which are pure Celtic. '*Blen*', which is found embedded in such place names as Blennerhasset, Blencow and Blaenau Ffestiniog in Wales, is the Celtic word for a 'rocky top'. Similarly the word '*pen*', meaning a 'headland', we find in Penrith, Penruddock, Penton, and, again in Wales, in Penmaenmawr.

The Anglian era, in the seventh and eighth centuries, brought words like *fluke*, meaning a 'flat-fish', from the Anglian word *flock*, and *gavelock,* a 'crowbar', a dialect word in use today but originating from the Anglian word, *gafeluc*. The well-known word *owt* for 'anything' and *nowt* for 'nothing' come from the Anglian words *awit* and *nawit*. As the Yorkshire expression goes '*if tha does owt for nowt tha does it for thissen*' ('if you do anything for nothing, you do it for yourself'). In fact, it's a phrase that's used right throughout the north of England, not just Yorkshire, and one we use in Cumbria as well. But above all, what shaped today's Wigton and Cumbrian English was the effect of the Norse language brought to the shores of the North West by the Vikings.

Melvyn Bragg picked up the point that Norse words live on today:

These words describe things that we recognise in our daily lives; it's a speech that exists to-day, that is spoken in the streets, that is spoken in the school playground, that is spoken by a lot of people in this town of five thousand people still. It's a living, vivid language, not a little folk memory. People don't have to dress up to say it; it really exists now, giving Cumbrian its distinctive savour, a whole lexicon of daily words like to *flit* – to move, a *cleg* – a horsefly, *gate* – not a gate but a thoroughfare (a gate is a *yet!*). As mentioned above, *yem* or *yam* means home; a *yek* is an oak and *gangin* means going. Then there are Norse-based terms that are less current but full of flavour and fairly breathe their antiquity, like *reave*, meaning to 'split', or *forelders*, meaning parents or ancestors – *foreldri* in Old Norse. And there are hundreds more.

Also, in Wigton itself, there are a lot of tinkers who've settled here and Irish families. Because of the gypsy encampments around here for so many years, we have a lot of Romany words too. For example, a word like *barry*, meaning good. 'That's barry', you'll hear that all the time in Wigton and *cady* for a hat, *chaver* for a boy, *pagger* meaning you're really winded, you're tired – *tha's paggered. Togs*, for clothes, is actually a Romany word. *Lure*, we still use up here, meaning money. Words like *swill* meaning a swill basket. Gypsies made them actually. They're made of reeds. My mother used to buy them off gypsies and used to put her washing in them. These words are probably only found in certain areas of Cumbria, areas where gypsies, tinkers traditionally gathered. The Rosley Hill fair, for example, just four or five miles from Wigton, was an important event in the area.

And one of the things that fascinates me, *says Bill Rollinson*, is that, here in Cumbria, we have a number of Scandinavian runic inscriptions written in the stick-like alphabet that the Scandinavians used to inscribe on stone and wood. But the fascinating thing is that all these inscriptions date from the early medieval period, from the twelfth to the thirteenth century, which suggests that if we were writing a Norse language in the thirteenth century, we were also still speaking a Norse language in the thirteenth century.

You do not have to look far to find evidence of the connections that still exist between twentieth century Wigton talk and these Norse influences that helped shape it a thousand years earlier. **Bill Rollinson** tells a true story from the 1940s from a little village called Flookburgh in the south of Cumbria. A young man called Harold Manning was sent to Iceland when the Allies occupied that country in 1940. Manning did not speak a word of Icelandic, yet within a week, using his own dialect words from Flookburgh, he managed to make himself understood. That is not to say that he could carry on a conversation with the people on whom he was billeted, but he could make himself understood by using his dialect words, which is really quite remarkable.

Melvyn Bragg tells a similar story, this time from Norway:

I went to Norway a few years ago – Bragg's a Norwegian name, Bragi – (he's a minor Norse god of poetry and war, incidentally, which I have always enjoyed); so I went to Norway to see if anybody looked like my relatives and I couldn't find anybody who did. But I was in this very nice hotel in Norway, in a really beautiful place up on a fjord where the Norwegian royal family take their holidays, and on a Saturday night these extremely grand people came, very well dressed and splendid-looking to have dinner.

Now you've got to remember that in Wigton speaking broad was frowned upon, slightly at home, certainly at school, and it was the rougher lads like myself who spoke very strongly. So, there I was in this exotic Norwegian resort, sitting in the dining room and this stunningly beautiful woman stood up and said 'Aas gannin yam!' Now that's what they say in Wigton. 'Aas gannin yam!'– I'm going home'. And I looked round amazed because it was as if I had gone back to Wigton: the incongruity of this woman speaking Wigton dialect was wonderful. It was a sort of marvellous cross-cultural thing, because in Wigton she would be regarded now as being a bit rough, really. Yet, there she was, a leading light of Fjord Society somewhere in Norway. And to hear that beautifully dressed woman speak as a very rough boy, namely me, would have spoken in Wigton fifty years ago, is an extraordinary leap, and this woman was speaking a language which is very near the roots of the Old English of this part of the world a thousand years ago.

The Anglo Saxons had been established in this part of Cumbria since the seventh or eighth century, while in the Cumbrian mountains there were communities of displaced

Britons, pushed out by the Anglo Saxons. There would have been a reasonable knowledge of Scottish Gaelic in the area, leaching down over the border from Scotland to the North and from the Irish across the Irish Sea. The nearby town of Whitehaven was a great magnet for Irish settlers who brought their own language and there was a lot of interchange between the English North West and Ireland around the end of the tenth century so there certainly would have been knowledge of Celtic in Cumbria at the time.

At the other end of the time-line encompassed by this book, Wigtonians today are just as connected to the outside world as anywhere else in the UK, and it is a point of honour that the folk who go from the town's big factory to work at their German subsidiary are up to the mark in German too. The modern vocabulary of English, then, that we call upon to describe our home and our locality, our local world, needs to be able to embrace the complexities that our lives throw up on a daily basis. This may involve work routines; there are thousands of specialist vocabularies to accommodate the technical specialities of particular jobs, from bricklayers to bishops, but also the regular functions of domestic life. It's not just chat round the house, here, but the greater complexities that technology has made familiar to us – fast-forward, spin-speed, freeze-dried... So how does our vocabulary measure up, compared with the Wigtonian's of a thousand years ago? Certainly it is larger. A thousand years of new things have collected around us, a thousand years of social and political development, of thought and reasoning, of discovery and exploration.

But, at the same time as the world has turned, the terms have turned with it. No longer do we use on a daily basis the specialist lexicon of the rural dweller, familiar with whippletrees and all the other paraphernalia of horse-hoeing husbandry. The eleventh

century farmer around Wigton was not short of words to describe his world. His vocabulary would have been reasonably large because the Old English vocabulary wasn't as big as that of modern English. It hadn't had the global expansion or the influence of French words. But if you were a tenant farmer in Wigton you would know quite a lot of words to do with your farm and the implements you used. Then, if you came into contact with the fishermen, you would know a lot of seafaring terms, and the same with the traders and so on. The largest vocabulary, however, would belong to those who were educated, that is to say, the local clergy.

As we have seen, the speech of Wigton remains rich and often impenetrable to outsiders, almost as substantial a linguistic barrier to mutual comprehension between different parts of the country as it must have been a thousand years ago. Yet, of course, Wigtonians must make themselves understood. Communications are intense and world wide, and it is no longer sufficient to be able to make yourself understood to your fellow farm-workers, or to your mates in the Public Bar of the 'Blackie' or the 'Sun' or even to the visiting horse-dealer passing through the town once a week or a month.

Wigtonians still like to speak broad in some situations, and that applies just as much to the teenage students of the local Nelson Thomlinson School sixth form – the same schoo that Melvyn Bragg attended forty-five years ago – as to the old hands. What they do is 'code-switch'. 'Code-switching' is linguists' jargon for what we all do from time to time to a certain extent; that is, vary the way we speak to suit different circumstances. Witness the differences between the talk of a pair of teenage girls discussing on the telephone, say, their plans for the weekend and the sudden 'switch' that occurs when the conversation is interrupted by a parent. The mode of address, the short-hand expressions, the actual range of vocabulary all change.

And it is code-switching that occurs, too, when Tony Blair turns on the matey charm to talk to Des O'Connor on television, or when people are accused of unnaturally 'talking posh'.

For the sixth-formers of Nelson Thomlinson, a capacity for code-switching will be essential. They have plans for university courses to be taken up at colleges well beyond the Danelaw, where they will need to modify what comes naturally to the tongue simply to make themselves understood to their tutors and room-mates. For them in the future there will be little room for the subtleties of the local speech they use at the moment.

One boy, for example, comes from Aspatria (pronounced *Spaytree*), near Workington and has a very distinct accent, his class-mates say, markedly different from standard 'Wigtonian'. It shows another set of linguistic contrasts with the speech of Workington, which is different again from Carlisle, only ten miles away to the north. The young people are proud of their talk, but see it as representing an 'older' form of expression and, as one student said: 'you do have to adjust the way you speak when you talk to somebody: I went to Oxford to look round the university and I felt bad in a way using my accent because you feel you've got to talk more southern to make yourself understood'. Because they won't

stay in the area, but will probably move away, they can't keep their accents. They'll be mixing with people where they are and they've got to make it easier for people around them to understand.

These young people from Wigton are still steeped in the sounds and vocabulary of the Cumbria they grew up in, yet perfectly able to code-switch to a more standard English in order to talk to visitors like Melvyn Bragg. Will they gradually lose their local voice, their Wigtonian identity?

One girl said "I think we'll always have it; we'll always have Cumbrian underneath. We'll just adapt. Put yourself in different surroundings and you just adapt your language straight away, but come back to Cumbria and you'll easily pick up the Cumbrian dialect – because it's within you.' But another is more pessimistic. She is sensitive to the gradual attrition of the stronger forms of the local speech: 'If you talk to my grandad you

Carnivals were a frequent event in local social life. This float celebrates Redmayne's Tailors, based in Wigton. They had over 60 shops all over the North, but all the work was done in Wigton. 'There's something in the make' was their slogan and they prided themselves on suits costing no more than 29/11d (today's £1.50p). Melvyn Bragg's mother worked there.

really wouldn't have a clue what he was saying, because he can't change his accent to sound more like 'standard English'. Cumbrian is the only way he knows; he has his own words for different things – he was a farmer and a lot of the farmers around here have their own words. For example, if he went down to the auction and you listened to him talking you wouldn't have a clue what they were saying and even I have trouble understanding him. He says things like '*get that yet oppin*' – meaning 'Open that gate!' Or then again '*Pick up that strier wi 't' gripe*' which means 'Pick up that straw with the (three-pronged) fork'. It's just normal for people to talk like that around here. We don't realise we're doing it and we don't think we're any different from anyone else. But I would never say something like '*Pick up that strier wi' t' gripe'*. It's the kind of language that is sort of dying out really because we don't – we can't – use it. You wouldn't hear one of us say gripe really. It's all going to die out, I think."

As **Professor Wales** has said:

Cumbria is remote from London, which has always been the centre of the country, and is surrounded by the Pennines and the Cumbrian mountains. People today who live there may never want to leave the place, but if you talk to them, they say they appreciate that it is remote. I remember reading Daniel Defoe's '*Tour through the whole island*' in which he describes different parts of Great Britain. He found this part of the world scary. A lot of people who went to the Lakes in the eighteenth century, thought they were beautiful and wild, but Defoe thought that they were the wildest most barren and frightful of any kind that he'd passed over in England – that kind of comment. The advantage, of course, is that in Cumberland and parts of the North, much much more than the South, you do find this wonderful heritage of regional speech.

WINC

2

HESTER

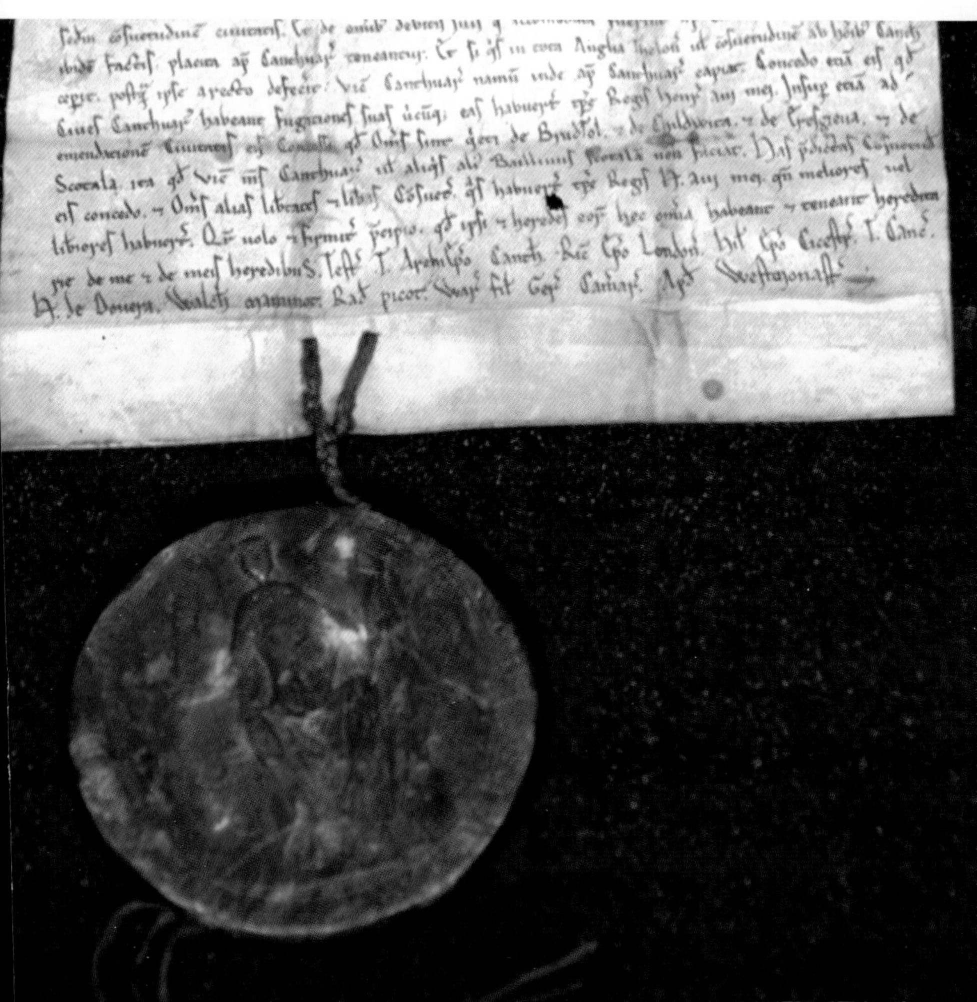

To visit Winchester today is to get caught up in the tangle of ring roads, one-way systems and parking horrors that seem to beset all our historic cathedral cities. In fact, the best way to get close to the ancestral heart of the city is by train. The short walk from the station to the Cathedral, the burial-place of Saxon Kings, where six great mortuary chests, including that of King Canute line the walls, passes through streets with much of their medieval fabric still intact.

It is now difficult to remember that Winchester was for nearly 200 years the nation's capital, the home of Kings and cradle of the English language. In the eleventh century Winchester English **was** English. Now, the voices to be heard on the streets are likely to be largely the grey tones of London washing away the Hampshire individuality of this essentially country town. When Melvyn Bragg, and Dr Kathryn Lowe of the University of Glasgow, visited a primary school to learn how Winchester's youngsters learn English, the accents of Hampshire were barely noticeable. The same day they met a young man who runs discos over half of southern England. He spoke proudly of his roots in Hampshire, yet he spoke with no sign of the local dialect. You had to step back one generation further and talk to his mother – who claimed with conviction to be 'a Hampshire Hog' – to hear at least an echo of the true local speech.

Only when they went to St Mary Magdalene Almshouses to talk to nonagenarian Arthur Dillow, who has been a baker in Winchester all his life, did they hear the true sound of Hampshire. One of a dwindling band of survivors of his era, he feels deeply the loss of real local speech, like the rasped Hampshire 'r' that rings out of his pronunciation 'OxfoRd' and 'BouRnemouth'. "Now it's Ox-fud and Bawn-muth", he snarls dismissively. How often, through the ages, have people in Winchester exclaimed at this sort of language change.

Barbara York is an Anglo-Saxon historian who has worked on Wessex and Anglo-Saxon kingship in particular. Melvyn Bragg met her at the Cathedral and asked her what Winchester would have been like a thousand years ago. She explained:

Winchester would be one of the larger towns in the country, and it would have been particularly dominated by its religious houses. One of the first things you'd see when you came into it was almost a quarter of the town given up to three religious houses. Then you'd be struck by the busy commerce in many parts of the city, particularly round the High Street – lots of shops and stores and probably quite a variety of accents. People would come from not only all over Wessex, but from other areas of Europe as well, to trade.

It's very difficult to give the exact size of the population at this time. A rough estimate would be six to eight thousand people, which doesn't sound very much these days, but many people in Anglo-Saxon England would be quite surprised to see that number of people. The three religious houses were the Old Minster, the New Minster, and the Nunnerminster. The Old Minster was the original Cathedral church and the present Winchester Cathedral is its successor. The New Minster that lay next to it was the house in which King Alfred was originally buried until he was moved out of town to Hyde Abbey. The Nunnerminster was founded by Alfred's wife when she retired in Winchester after his death. That, too, was a very vibrant

community. There were two particular saints, local saints – St Swithun, who was the Old Minster saint, and Eadburgha who was the main saint of Nunnerminster, and was a granddaughter of King Alfred.

The Cathedral in which we're talking to each other now would not have been built then and none of the religious houses would be anything like the size of the Cathedral. The churches would be much smaller but quite intricate and very, very highly decorated. They would make quite an impression on anyone who saw them.

Winchester was well known for its wealth and culture and the three houses would certainly make a great impression on a visitor. There was probably also a royal palace just opposite the Cathedral, and it would be the range of houses and buildings in the city as a whole which would impress people. It wouldn't just be any old shops and stores, you'd get some quite specialist people – goldsmiths, silversmiths, making for the elite of the country. And when walking around the cathedral area, you'd also see the burial places of a number of the elite, with wonderful gravestones, proclaiming their names and status so that nobody could mistake them.

It was also a centre of education a thousand years ago. That would be based in the religious houses, but all three of the Minsters would have children educated in them as well as people who might come in to take up their profession rather later. They would be centres of scholarship – particularly the Old Minster and the New Minster. We know a number of works that can be related to them.

A lot of the children coming to school would be local, but quite well connected locally. Because a lot of the Winchester clergy had national connections with the whole hierarchy of the English Courts. It was quite prestigious to be entered at somewhere like the Old Minster in Winchester or even the Nunnerminster in Winchester, so one would expect a bigger pool of people. Entry

often depended on birth rather than on qualifications.

To learn more about the educational tradition of Winchester, Melvyn Bragg and Dr. Kathryn Lowe of Glasgow University, began their journey back to the roots of Old English speech by focusing on a dialogue – an imagined conversation – composed towards the end of the first millennium. The author who caught something of the cadences of eleventh-century speech was a Benedictine monk from Winchester named Ælfric whose job it was to teach young boys. He was very good at reaching out to his pupils who would probably have been aged

diabolo siue inimicis meis uisibilibus tradar . Sed tu potius

bone xpe in misericordia tua . & non in furore corripe me

Et ubi cumqʒ oberrauero a te . reuoca me ad te . Atqʒ reuoca(ns)

paterna pietate semp custodi ad gloriam nominis tui . qd sit

benedictu in secula . AMEN .

Nos pueri rogamus te magister ut doceas nos loqui latial(iter)
recte quia idiote sumus & corrupte loquimur . Quid uultis
loqui? quid curamus . quid loquamur nisi recta locutio sit
& utilis non anilis aut turpis . Vultis flagellari in discendo
Carius est nobis flagellari p(ro)doctrina quam nescire . Sed sc(imus)
te mansuetu esse & nolle inferre plagas nobis nisi cogar(is)
a nobis . Interrogo te quid mihi loqueris? quid habes ope
pressus sum monachu & psallam omni die septe sinaxes cu fra(tribus)
& occupatus sum lectionibus & cantu . sed tamen uelle in(ter)
discere sermocinari latina lingua . Quid sciunt isti tui soci(i)
Alii sunt aratores . alii opiliones . quidam bubulci . quidam e(tiam)
uenatores alii piscatores . alii aucupes . quidam mercatores . q(ui)
dam sutores . quidam salinatores . Quidam p(i)stores loci . Quid
dicis tu arator? Quomodo exerces opus tuu? Omni die mu(ltum)
laboro exeo diluculo minando boues ad campu & iungo e(os)
ad aratru non est tam aspa hiemps ut audea latere don(i)
pro more dni mei sed iunctis bobus & confirmato uomere
& cultro aratro omni die debeo arare integru agru au(t)

This is the beginning of Ælfric's *Colloquy*. The work, written in Latin, is designed for young boys to practise their Latin, broaden their vocabulary and develop their conversation skills. The *Colloquy* is structured as a dialogue, where pupils would adopt the roles of individuals working in different occupations and answer questions on their day's work by the master. At the bottom of the page, for example, the 'ploughman' is explaining that he has to plough an acre a day no matter how severe the winter. The *Colloquy* was produced at the end of the tenth century while Ælfric was school master at the monastery of Cerne Abbas in Dorset. Above the text you can see writing in a different smaller hand. This is in Old English and translates the Latin word for word. In the middle of the last line you may be able to make out the Latin verb-form *debeo*, which s glossed '*ic sceal*' ('I must').

Three copies of the text survive.

between seven and fifteen. He wrote three series of homilies and saints' lives, biblical paraphrases and several further minor works, including a grammar of Latin which is explained in Old English. This was an innovative idea in those days and tells us a lot about Ælfric. He was worried about the lack of Latin literacy and therefore the confusion among the clergy about Christian principles. He wanted to make scripture understandable to clergy and laymen and thought that a grammar, explained through the vernacular, would make it easier for monks and nuns and anyone who could read to understand the Latin texts and therefore comprehend the Christian faith. He also produced a glossary, so that once the students had learned the grammar they could use the glossary to build up their vocabulary.

He wrote his *Colloquy* as a teaching tool in Latin. It was a set conversation piece between a teacher and his pupils which was a device often used for teaching grammar, vocabulary and correct pronunciation. It is particularly interesting to us now because, over the top of the Latin words, someone has written a rough version in Old English. We cannot be sure that it was written by Ælfric himself, but it does fit in with his purpose. It cannot reproduce the cadences of everyday Anglo-Saxon speech because it follows the Latin word order, but it gives us some idea of the language at the time,

Ælfric was born in Wessex and lived between 995 and 1010. He is important because he wrote on a wide range of topics often in Old English when everyone else was using Latin. He was a protege of a man called Bishop Æthwold, who did much to develop the religious and political life of the Church and he himself was a prolific author and translator. One of his themes is the usefulness to society of all sorts and conditions of men, using the simple ploughman, on whom everyone depends for their food, as a symbol. It was a symbol often used in the literature of the time. His *Colloquy* is clear and fairly simple, using repetition and alliteration and frequent references to his audience to draw his hearers into the sermon. In this way he gives us some idea of the things which were important in Anglo Saxon life. **Dr. Lowe** talked about Ælfric and his methods of teaching to Melvyn Bragg:

We think that the *Colloquy* would have been written at some stage in the 980s, after Ælfric left Winchester for Cerne Abbas. Ælfric was in fact trying to teach Latin, but he did so in the language of English. There's nothing new there. What's new is how he managed to make his students be excited by the language, by shrouding Latin grammar and Latin vocabulary in a conversation, quite a lively conversation. A colloquy is a dialogue between his master and his pupils. How Ælfric adapted this technique was by assigning each of his pupils a role. And he took occupations of social classes that we really don't learn anything about in Anglo-Saxon England. For example, one of his pupils might be a ploughman for the day, and then Ælfric's master would ask that pupil what the ploughman did when he got up and what his job was like. And so it would go on – one's a ploughman, one's a fisherman, and one's a monk himself. It gives people a chance, in other words, to exercise their vocabulary and practise their Latin grammar. Before that colloquies had tended to be a little bit like phrase books, and really not very interesting. Ælfric changed that.

We really don't know much about the teaching of English per se. What we do know about is the teaching of Latin because it was important for monks to know Latin, not simply because many of their texts were in Latin, but because they would have to go abroad, and they would have to converse with people from the Continent. The way they did this was through Latin. We read the *Colloquy* today in Old English – that's its importance for us – but it should be remembered that, in fact, the *Colloquy* is in Latin, and the Old English itself isn't the Old English of Ælfric – it was probably put together by a man also called Ælfric – Ælfric Barter – who was Ælfric's only

A map showing where invasions from different parts of the Continent brought new ideas and new languages to Britain.

known pupil. We certainly know that Barter made adaptations.

We need to realise that Old English goes much further back than that. Our first writings in Old English are from the seventh century. So we're picking up the story in a sense halfway through, but it's quite right to start with Ælfric because Ælfric is of fundamental importance to the history of Old English. He was a most prolific writer and his books on saints' lives were sort of popular novels of the day because sometimes saints died in quite remarkable, and sometimes quite gory, ways.

His works were copied across the country, into a standard literary language, which we know today as late West Saxon. It was another three, four hundred years before we saw another standard, a standard based on London, which essentially became the predecessor of modern day English. The language of Ælfric is certainly the first standard one in English, but we mustn't forget people like King Alfred, who had a whole programme of educational reform. To an extent, Ælfric was building on that, but he took it a little bit further. He devised a grammar and a glossary, so that people could actually learn Latin, whereas Alfred was interested more in translation programmes.

When only a small proportion of the population could understand Latin, the language of official documents often had to be mixed. Another example of the way in which they had to be written both in Old English and Latin was described by **Michael Stansfield**, an archivist of the period. He talked about an Anglo-Saxon charter dated 937, but probably written much later, some parts of which were written in Latin and some in Old English:

The first part of the document is in Latin and it starts off with a formal invocation and a quotation from the Book of Ecclesiastes, on the lines of vanity, vanity, all is vanity. Then it says who is granting what and to whom. That is followed by the description of the boundaries of the

land and, at that point, the document goes from Latin into Anglo Saxon or Old English. The boundary is described in Old English and it's quite possible that this is so that the man in the street would actually understand and know what were the boundaries of the land that were being granted, because that is what would effect him most pertinently.

The document would quite possibly have been read out. It would formally have been agreed in the Church, perhaps laid on the altar in the Cathedral, and then all the people who are recorded as having witnessed the document would actually have come along. There's a cross alongside the name of each witness at the bottom and they would have touched that cross and that would have been their act of witnessing the document. Then, after that formal ceremony, if you like, it would quite possibly have actually been read out in the street to the people who would have needed to know about the boundaries and would have been affected by the change of land owner.

Other ways had to be found of recording business transactions between people who could

art of an early wall painting in Winchester Cathedral
epicting Christ being taken down from the cross and
ails being removed from his feet. Painted at a time
hen not everyone could read, the ideas of the
hristian religion were often conveyed to people
rough stained glass windows and wall paintings.

 one time pilgrims used to go to Winchester in large
umbers, but when Canterbury and the shrine of
homas à Becket became popular fewer people visited.

not read. **Michael Stansfield** also described a tally stick which would be used to keep track
of accounts:

**We have a wooden tally stick, dated from about fourteen hundred. It's just a long, thin strip of
wood which has got about five or six notches in it, which would indicate the amount in
question. This is a financial record, so, when you paid your account or whatever, this tally
would be made, these notches would be cut and then it's split in two down the middle and I
would keep one half as my receipt and the accountant or whatever would keep the other half
as their receipt. Some of them come with addresses and names written on them but this one
is quite plain. And there would have been an awful lot of these around in the Middle Ages. If
you look at almost any Medieval account it will say, 'paid by tally' and that would have been a
transaction involving one of these documents.**

Literacy is one of the fundamental factors determining the quality of life at all levels of
society. When Alfred became King of Wessex in 871 the state of learning in England was at
a low point, partly as a result of the effect on English scholarship and monastic learning
which the Danish raids were having. Their raids had been going on since 787 and were
particularly destructive in Northumbria, not only threatening the lives and livelihoods of the
ordinary people but plundering the great and famous monasteries of Northumbria which
had been the centre of learning in the country. The Danes sacked the monasteries, ripping
up the precious manuscript books which had been gathered there and murdering the
monks or driving them away.

hey had then begun to settle in the eastern and northern parts of the country, particularly
ound York and Lincolnshire where there are over 1,500 place names of Scandinavian
rigin. Over 600 names end in *−by* which is the Danish word for settlement or town, or

43

sometimes simply farm, so places like Derby, Grimsby and others were originally Danish strongholds. Other endings like –*thorpe* meaning, village , or –*thwaite* which means an isolated area or –*toft* which simply means a piece of ground are also very common in those areas of the North or eastern Midlands which the Danes took over. The –*thwaite* ending has also got tagged on to family names, since people were often called, originally, by the name of the place from which they came. A man from Braithwaite, for instance, would be known simply by that name when he travelled to another village. The Danes also had a habit of tacking –*son* on to first names to indicate family groupings. A lot of surnames ending in –*son* , such as Henderson or Davidson, are found in this area and most of these had a Danish origin a long way back.

Although Alfred had defeated the Danes, as the Anglo-Saxon Chronicle tells us, in a series of decisive battles in 878 and kept them out of Wessex for a hundred years, the peace only lasted until 991. Danish invasions and victories then forced the English King Ethelred into exile and the country came under Danish rule. Winchester, the royal and ecclesiastical

ft: Winchester Cathedral is a cruciform structure which was begun in 1079 and finished in the sixteenth
entury. The character of the building was originally pure Norman, and the transept and central tower, built
Bishop Walkelyn, are admirable specimens of that style. The Cathedral contains the remains of many of
e Kings of Wessex and of the Saxon Kings of England.

elow: The Library in Winchester Cathedral. with books recording church matters and two early globes. The
urch was the main repository of written knowledge until about 500 years ago. As a result, churches and
thedrals in large towns often carry records of title deeds, births, deaths and marriages – functions now
rried out by civil registrars. Those wishing to study the social history of an area often start with church
cords.

centre of Wessex, began to lose its influence.

In a conversation with Melvyn Bragg, **John Hardacre**, the Curator at Winchester Cathedral, emphasised the importance of King Alfred's Court and its relationship to the Church:

The Kings had what was called a crown wearing ceremony. They came every Easter to wear their crown in Winchester. There was a great symbiosis of Church and State. The King got his authority from the Church and the Church got its momentum from the King and this is just typical of Winchester in the tenth century.

This symbiosis between Church and State was really begun by King Alfred. It was he who realised that the state of learning in the country had reached such a sorry state in the ninth century. Very, very few people could read and write Latin. It was his cultural renaissance in Winchester – the establishment of schools, the importing of craftsmen and scholars from Wessex and Mercia and the Continent – that really built up a culture of learning, and began to equip the country with the basic literacy from which everything else derives.

The scribes in the monasteries would have been working very hard in this period which was one of great literary activity. A large number of poems in Old English were composed and circulated and although, or perhaps because, standards of Latin scholarship were low, English as a language developed greater flexibility and range and generally gained in power and prestige at this time. When we think of King Alfred as 'the light of a benighted age' we think not only of things like establishing the navy or working out a way of telling the time – or even the burning of the cakes – we think also of the literary and cultural renaissance which he encouraged.

Although we have got some idea of the lives of people in this period through their literature we have very little clear idea about the ways in which Scandinavian words mixed in with Ol

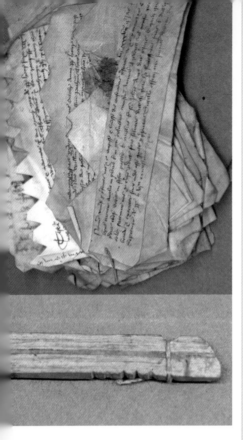

The Battle of Maldon

Feoll þa to folden fealohilte swurd:
ne mihte he gehealdan heardne mece,
wæpnes wealdan. þa gyt þaet word gecwæð
har hilderinc, hyssas bylde,
bæd gangan forð gode geferan.

This passage comes from a famous Old English poem known as *The Battle of Maldon*. It was composed to commemorate the deaths of many Anglo-Saxons and their noble leader in a real life skirmish against the Vikings in AD 991.

Some of the words look unfamiliar because we no longer have some of the letter forms in our modern alphabet. þ (known as 'thorn') and ð ('eth') both represent 'th', so *forð* in the extract is simply FORTH. *æ* ('ash') is pronounced in present day English as the 'a' is in 'apple'. This should make *þaet* recognisable as THAT. Reading aloud many of these words will suggest their modern equivalents: *swurd* is SWORD, *heardne* HARD, *waepne* WEAPON, *wealdan* WIELD, *feoll* FELL, *word* WORD, *gode* GOOD. It should also emphasise Old English poetry's most characteristic feature: its use of alliteration. You will hear that in each line two or three words start with the same sound. Another characteristic of Old English poetry is its use of synonyms (or near synonyms); this poem uses a variety of expressions for nouns like 'warrior', battle or 'sword'. Many of these are not found in prose of the same period. Much of this variation is used for alliterative purposes, although it can also have a dramatic stylistic effect. Here in this extract the leader, Byrhtnoth (who has just been fatally wounded by the Vikings), is described as *har hilderinc* a 'grey-haired battle-warrior'. His men are his *hyssas* 'warriors', although over fifty other words are recorded with the same basic meaning!

Here is a translation of the passage:
Then the golden-hilted sword fell to the ground, he (Byrhtnoth) could not hold the hard sword, wield the weapon. Still the grey-haired battle-warrior made a speech, he encouraged his warriors, bade his good companions go forth.

English words and what the language actually sounded like. Since, particularly on the borders of Wessex, people of Scandinavian origin were living alongside people who spoke Old English, presumably they must have developed some sort of common language in order to trade with each other. Judging by Ælfric's Colloquy, Old English was gaining ground and being used in the monasteries. Winchester might be a centre for Latin scholarship, but Latin could not compete with Old English in everyday conversation. By the time Winchester ceased to be the centre of civilisation in Southern England, English was established as a powerful language.

HA

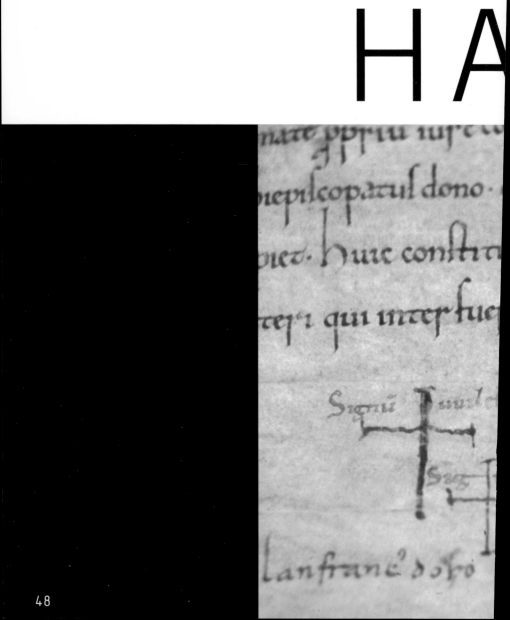

STINGS 3

uriam uel ubi cantuariensi archiepo

consenserunt prefatus rex & arch

episcopi.

...regine.

ensis archiepis subscripsit

There are few places in Britain more associated, in name at least, with France than the Sussex town of Hastings. Needless to say, it is the place that gave its name to the battle that defined relations between the English and French nations, a defeat for the English that has ever since epitomised the state of intense rivalry, sometimes of bitter enmity, that has marked how the two nations have regarded each other. Most British schoolchildren who know anything about the subject know also that the Battle of Hastings – the triumph of William the First that brought Norman kings to the throne of England – was actually fought not at Hastings itself but on the site of the nearby village of Battle.

At Hastings, in 1066, the course of English history changed. It brought new ways of governing the country and new ways of speaking. Hastings looks towards France, less than 30 miles away across the Channel. It is a convenient arrival point from the Continent, whether for friends or enemies, so welcome and wariness have traditionally been blended together. With French and English fishermen setting out from opposite sides of the channel to find the best fish, there have always been quarrels, but there

Previous page:
This is the Accord of Winchester, a document signed in 1072 in which the Archbishop of York acknowledges the supremacy of the Archbishop of Canterbury that still is valid today. It is signed by those involved and by those who were witnesses. At the top the King, William the Conquerer, has put his mark, an upright cross, and followed by his wife, Matilda with her mark and signature. The King of England could not read or write being a working, that is, fighting king. The sword was mightier than the pen in those days.

Left: The gateway to the Abbey at Battle commemorating the most significant battle in the history of England in which the French King William I, defeated the English King Harold. From this battle stemmed a new form of government, new cultural values and, most importantly, new ways of speaking.

have also been times when fishermen from both sides have worked alongside each other, mingling French and English words through necessity and making a bridge between the two languages. While he was in Hastings Melvyn Bragg talked to **Dennis Collins**, a local historian, about this rivalry:

There's been a continual state of confrontation, amiable – or not so amiable – almost since the Norman period. The English and French have fought at Hastings on several occasions both on the sea and on land. Mostly they've fought about fishing. In the sixteenth century and seventeenth centuries there were innumerable battles in which the two sides used to raid each other's towns and ships, capture the fishermen and hold each other to ransom. Sometimes English sailors were tortured by the French who caught them. And all the time, of course, they were all busily smuggling to and fro. It's said that just along the coast was a gentleman who provided Napoleon with his English newspapers every day, but if you ask the fishermen which of the other fishermen they don't get on with they say 'the French, because they're still raiding the fishing grounds' as they were in 1561 when there was a big ordinance to try and stop them. And it's just gone on.

Some of the place names around Hastings also reflect the close language ties between France and England. There is a part of Hastings known as Rock-a-Nore. I could never make out why Rock-a-Nore Road – 'a road to the north' – should be considered interesting enough to be called that. The truth is that to the English it wasn't, but to the French it was, and just past it on the cliff there is a thing called Foul Lace which of course is *falaise* which is French for cliff. Although the French and English have often suffered at each others' hands, they have also had common interests. Throughout the years, in the smuggling which took place twice a month in the dark of the moon, the English were busily dealing with the French. It was an entire industry which was going on.

However, in spite of its proximity to France, there is very little to suggest France about the modern seaside resort of Hastings. In fact, it has the quintessentially English aspect of a gentle south coast town with its broad promenade, the statutory array of souvenir shops interspersed with chippies and that other essential adjunct to today's British seaside experience, the shopping centre. Hastings has a faded gentility, too, not so grand as Brighton, a bit raffish, but without its zippier neighbour's streak of fashionable defiance of convention.

Not that Hastings is down at heel. On a summer morning it operates its holiday machine efficiency in that curiously British way, quite unlike the continental notion of *les vacances au bord de la mer*. Instead of a name with a quaint ending in –ville, or –on–sea that might promise a leisurely day on the sea front, Hastings with its strange 'ings' at the end, suggesting hasty weddings or noisy hustings, takes its name from a local tribe, the *Haestingas* back in the Dark Ages. They were the followers of *Haesta*, a warrior who, in turn, got his name from the Old English word for 'violence' *haest*. This apparently peaceful town has fought hard for its peace.

It is still an uncertain peace. When, in a recent move to brighten up the town, a decision was taken to display flags, including the colours of William ('the Conqueror') of Normandy, there was considerable resistance. And the idea of the French as 'the old enemy' dies hard amongst those who must share trading territory. As **Dennis Collins** said:

An old fisherman I was talking to recently said they (the French) were the real trouble. Hastings people get on with everybody along the coast pretty well, but if we have any real trouble, they say, it's always with the French, they come and pinch our fishing zone. So people have got long

memories in Hastings and they do care – there is a still a feeling that France is the old enemy.

However, it is the shared history of the two nations, across times of conflict, conquest, alliance and through trading links, that has helped produce the indelible effect French has had on the English language:

You imagine a set of English fishermen who probably couldn't even write and a set of French fishermen, both busily smuggling on a dark night, you know, they're going to pick up each other's words – it's almost impossible not to.

The Battle of Hastings that placed French speaking monarchs on the throne of England, had thus a decisive influence on our language. It was not that the conquered Saxons started speaking French – the language of the conqueror remained the language of the Court, while Old English continued to be spoken by the mass of the populace. What it did was fundamentally to influence English vocabulary.

The battle was perceived nationally as a huge tragedy. Scholars have argued about the immediate effect it had on people on different social levels, but they generally agree that people were stupefied by the defeat, and found it difficult to come to terms with the overthrow of the old system. New legal procedures and tax systems were introduced. For instance, new procedures were brought in to formalise the way villages paid tithes (taxes, usually in the form of corn which would be stored in tithe barns) to the Church according to their means. Possessions, including land and estates, were carefully valued and recorded in the *Domesday Book* and even the ordinary people understood that their place in society was being much more clearly defined than it had been in the past. The feudal system which placed everyone in a hierarchy of service, so that everyone, right up to the level of king, owed a duty to the person above them, laid the basis for a more formalised class society. **Frank McGlynn**, who has written extensively on the affairs of 1066, explained to Melvyn Bragg what lay behind the Norman intrusion into England:

The basic reason for the Norman Conquest was that William liked to bind powerful nobles to himself by grants of land. In Normandy there simply wasn't enough land, so much of the impetus behind the Conquest of England was to find more land for his powerful nobles who otherwise might have turned against him, whereupon Normandy might have been wrecked by a civil war. There's a kind of a geo-political imperative behind the invasion as well as William's own personal ambitions.

William probably did not expect to win so easily. He did so because Harold did this extremely stupid thing of committing all his forces and all his elite nobles in one battle. His brother, Garth, advised him firstly not to fight William at Hastings, and secondly not to commit all his men in one do or die confrontation. He said 'let me face William and you hang back in London, then if I lose, you can lead a second army'. But Harold ignored the advice and pressed on to fight William when his army were ill prepared and overtired. The problem about the Battle of Hastings was that the entire Anglo-Saxon military elite was destroyed in one fell swoop, leaving a complete vacuum in terms of leadership, and the only people who could have come forward as leaders were the northern earls who had their own separatist agenda and foolishly thought they could do a deal with William, whereby he retained the south of England and they retained the North. They were swiftly disillusioned on that score.

They were severely demoralised without any question and felt that they'd been let down by all the people they might have looked to for help. There were, of course, the occasional heroes such as Hereward the Wake in the Fens, but by and large they were leaderless and demoralised.

Morale is a very important thing in history and there was certainly a crisis of morale after 1066.

News of the defeat spread through the country by word of mouth surprisingly quickly, considering the primitive communications of the time. It was a remarkable event in that it all hinged on one battle, because usually in that era battles were not decisive in that way – they tended not to solve things. The slaughter in the battle also created something of a sensation throughout Europe, because the casualty levels and the general bloodshed was much greater than people were used to.

Another great change came in the need to adapt to the French language and culture. People would have had to speak French to be part of the Court, otherwise they just wouldn't have been understood. It was a practical consideration, it was also a social consideration. If you spoke Saxon, quite apart from not being understood, you didn't really come across as having much prestige or much power, so it was very much the combination of those two factors I think that led to a lot of the Saxon upper class learning Norman French very, very quickly. And then, of course, it would have filtered down to lower strata of Saxon society by a similar process. If you were hob-nobbing with people at Court, then that gave you a certain prestige and you wanted to show off about it, so you adopted some of their words which would have been Norman French words – words like *vin* or *mouton* or *appareil*.

English kings had always had close links with Normandy. Edward the Confessor, for instance, spoke French as a first language and spent much of his life in Normandy. When he became King of England, he surrounded himself with Norman courtiers so Norman French was a significant language at the English Court long before the invasion, even though English was still the main language. After the arrival of William the Conqueror, Norman French became the official language of the Court and no king of England spoke English as their first language for the next 300 years. Gradually, the key positions in English society and government were taken over by Normans rather than Anglo-Saxons. French-speaking craftsmen, scholars, designers and servants, such as cooks, were brought over from France, but the more menial jobs remained unchanged and the life of ordinary people went on much as before. However, it was only when Henry IV became King that England was ruled by someone whose language was English rather than French.

Only two or three percent of the population was Norman and that is a very small percentage. Norman French didn't become the language of England, but it infiltrated English as it was spoken at every level of society – so much so that by the time you're talking about English coming back, it's a very different English. It really is a hybrid language. It's still English because the things that we recognise languages by, such as the words for numbers or words like *the* are recognisably English, but the rest of the vocabulary has been transformed almost beyond recognition. Words like *hotel, hostelry, master* (developed from French *maître*) began to be widely used, as did those, with the originally Latin prefixes *mal* or *bon* or *ben*. Words like malicious, maiady, benefit and benevolent came in.

Whenever you have a society which is ruled by people speaking one language, however small that group is, then their language will tend to predominate in certain functions. After the Norman Conquest, French became the language of the Court and of administration. Even the motto of the Court '*Honi soit qui mal y pense*' (evil be to him who thinks evil) was in French and has remained so till this day. As there were so few Normans available to do all the administrative jobs, people from the native population did those jobs, becoming, as it were, civil servants. Therefore, they had to learn the language of power. There were a lot of people who were not only bilingual but probably changed language very often in their every day life, perhaps even in mid sentence. This is known as code-switching. Because of this, the language of the powerful will filter down and eventually become more familiar to people lower down the social hierarchy. It's a matter of prestige really and prestige is a great driving force with language change.

What it did was fundamentally to influence English vocabulary. English took in at least ten thousand loan words from French over the next two or three hundred years. Of course, a lot of them have subsequently disappeared, and several of them are quite rare, but there are thousands of French words which are commonly used in English today: *peace, battle, arms, siege, enemy, armour, religion, service, saint, miracle, clergy, sacrifice, chase, scent, falcon, quarry, forest, retrieve, design, beauty, music, romance, costume, garment, apparel, dress, train, petticoat....* Twenty-eight nouns, nouns that feel wholly and incontrovertibly English, and yet they represent a tiny fraction of the rich variety of English words that began as French. They tend to congregate in certain areas of meaning.

In the grounds of Hastings Castle Melvin Bragg and J.C. Smith of St Catherine's College, Oxford, discussed examples of this, talking about the areas in which French words were particularly prominent. For obvious reasons, a lot of words the French used for battles and fighting got mixed up with English and entered the language after 1066. Words like *battle, conquest and castle, arms, siege* are all good Norman French words, as are *lance* and *armour*. They were used alongside English words like *sword* and *spear*. Similarly, the French word *archer* was used alongside the English word *bowman* and more or less replaced it. Sometimes pairs of words, like French *liberty* and English *freedom*, were synonymous at first but gradually developed slightly different senses. Later on, as the terminology of fighting became more complex, words like *infantry, cav-alry* and *cannon* entered the language through French, although they are originally

57

Italian words derived from Latin. Since hunting was the other important activity for powerful men, many French words were employed to describe it. Words like *chase, scent, quarry, forest, falcon, retrieve* provided the basic vocabulary for hunting and also many of the technical terms in falconry which are still used today.

Many religious ideas were conveyed by French words. The word *religion* itself came to England from Normandy, as did words like *service, saint, miracle, clergy, sacrifice*, and many of the phrases used to describe ideals of chivalry or honour, which played such an important part in the culture of the time, are distinctly French.

But French also enlarged and influenced the way people spoke about more homely things. The language of food contains obvious examples. **J.C. Smith** talked to Melvyn Bragg about the influence of French on our culinary language as they munched their way through a plate of plaice and chips at Hastings' Mermaid restaurant:

The Mermaid's menu (both *menu* and *restaurant*, are, incidentally, French words that appeared in English during the nineteenth century, soon after they become fashionable in Paris) has many words for food that come from French: *plaice, pork, gammon, onion, peach* and *cream*, which are all medieval words. *Salad*, also on the Mermaid's menu, is a slightly later loan word, while *sorbet* and *croquettes* are much more recent imports. The more recent the borrowing from across the Channel, the less anglicised its spelling and pronunciation is likely to be. One thing that's not listed on the Mermaid's menu, but is to be found on its tables, (*table* is another French word, of course), is that staple of the fish and chip shop, vinegar. Vinegar is simply the old French word for sour wine – *vin aigre*.

There were two main factors that came into play in this linguistic adoption game: sometimes i was simply a question of novelty. The peach, for example, was not an indigenous English fruit

astings beach, looking out towards France. Now
pparently a typical English seafront, it was at this
each, or one close to it, that William the Conquerer
nded with his army in 1066.

so the term arrived with the people who grew and enjoyed it. The other major determinant was prestige. The Normans brought their taste in food and, as they were wealthy and held positions of power, their main experience of certain animals was in slices on a plate. The English peasant, on the other hand, reared animals but probably did not eat meat particularly frequently. It was, therefore, the Norman name of the animal that came to be associated, with its prestige, with food. Thus, we end up eating beef, pork, mutton and so on, whilst the old English words like pig and sheep continued to refer to the animal because it was reared by English speakers.

Apart from the language of the table, many words we use to describe furniture and objects in the home, such as *carpet, wardrobe, chair* are derived from French. The Normans set the fashion in design (another French word), so many basic architectural terms such as *joist* came from them. This link between vocabulary and design has lasted up to the present day. It's surprising how much terminology connected with motor cars and aeroplanes, words like *chassis, fuselage* and others, are originally French.

Another obvious area where French rules is the world of fashion. Words like *couture, garment, train, apparel, petticoat, costume* all owe their use to an admiration for French clothes, just as many words used to describe painting, music and sculpture reflect the English respect for, and interest in, French culture.

In contrast, almost no English weather terms are borrowed from French. Rain, wind, sun, snow, sleet, drizzle, hail, shower, cloud, mist, fog are all English words, not French. The reason is very obvious. The Normans may have brought a lot of things with them, but they didn't bring the weather.

Three distinct waves bring this tide of French words into English and they should not be confused. They came for subtly different reasons. The first wave was one of power

Panic was spreading through the French army followi
a rumour that William was dead. The King raises
visor to show his men he was still leading them. befc
his fortunes change

–words that came in with the Normans were actually brought here by people who invaded and conquered England. The second wave consists of words from Parisian as opposed to Norman French – not the same thing at all. There were, and are, varieties of French just as there were, and are, different sorts of English. Speakers of Parisian French never invaded Britain, but in the later Middle Ages their language acquired a certain prestige. What happened was that, paradoxically, just as Norman French was on the wane, Parisian French was on the increase as a prestige social language. Thus, in the thirteenth, fourteenth and fifteenth centuries we get words coming from that language which was never spoken in Britain.

It was the humorist, Miles Kington, who some twenty years ago, invented *Franglais* as a piece of linguistic *jeu d'esprit*, mixing English and French to produce a sort of witty mid-Channel soup. Yet the history of such linguistic stewpots is as old as language itself. And recent much-publicised attacks by the French language authorities (in the form of the *Académie Française*) on the supposedly pernicious influence of English on French – linguistic impurities – are by no means new. This sort of mélange is a style of language called macaronic, in which some elements are taken from each language.

Although English has been a very promiscuous language, borrowing words from a huge number of sources, it is important to realise that French also has drawn words from many sources. Exactly the same arguments that are currently being used against English words in French today by the *Académie Française* were used against the influx of Italian words in the sixteenth century.

And he points to another piece of amusing macaronic language that blends French and English in that other linguistically disputed territory, North America, where in the

Canadian province of New Brunswick there is a variety of so-called French, *Chiaque*, which contains sentences like, *'J'ai parké mon char au corner de la street'*. Today, international trade and the cultural and economic influence of North America on the world means that most of the linguistic currents are flowing from English into other languages. Yet, within Europe, French continues its influence on English, through the European Union. Because the European Market has been dominated by French-speaking countries (France, Belgium and Luxembourg) and by French law, many of the basic terms of European jurisprudence are still French. **J.C.Smith** commented:

Only the other day I read in the newspaper the word *acqui*, meaning what the community has achieved, what's been achieved so far. It's quite a common word in some E.U. circles. Similarly, the adjective *communautaire*, meaning 'Community-minded', or 'in the spirit of the Community' – of which there is no neat English equivalent – is also frequently used in certain legal registers of the language. Sometimes we get straight translations of French terms that sound very odd in English. One of my favourite examples is the French *viande ovine*, meaning, basically, lamb and mutton, which gets translated as sheep-meat in all the European directives.

As we saw above, sheep to a Saxon peasant was both an animal and also the name of its meat. When the Normans came, they ate the meat but didn't rear the animal. So they called what they ate 'mutton'. This produced the distinction between 'sheep', the animal raised by the peasant farmer and 'mutton', the meat eaten by the Norman Court. Then the term 'mutton' came to be thought rather derogatory – 'mutton' was tough old meat; 'mutton dressed as lamb'. So nowadays hardly anyone uses mutton

And sheep-meat of any age is called lamb. But we are left with this strange literal translation of *viande ovine* – sheep-meat – that has come to us through the European Community. French is giving way to English. Who knows where this will end.

CANT

RBURY

Canterbury has always been a place of pilgrimage. Ever since St Augustine arrived there in 579 it has been a symbol of Christianity and learning . As Geoffrey Chaucer wrote in the 1390s:

> Whan that Aprille, with hise shoures soote,
> The droghte of March hath perced to the roote
> And bathed every veyne in swich licour,
> Of which vertu engendred is the flour......
> Thanne longen folk to goon on pilgrimages…
> And specially, from every shires ende
> Of Engelond, to Caunturbury they wende,
> The hooly blisful martir for to seke
> That hem hath holpen, whan that they were seeke.

To ride to Canterbury today, unless you are peculiarly keen to take a circuitous scenic route, is to trundle into town on the A2 motorway. This delivers the modern pilgrim efficiently enough to the city centre, where the Cathedral tower rises above the cluttered medieval roofs, but then leaves you stranded. You find yourself caught up in skeins of no entrys and pedestrianised thoroughfares that defeat the motorist.

So for today's pilgrim, it's back to the car park to pay-and-display before joining the bobbing heads and cameras spilling through the narrow streets. Only the old black and white sign pointing one way to Rochester, the other to London, reminds us of an ancient way. Today's Canterbury sounds are likely to include a babble of French spoken by kids on a school trip from Calais, a   Mid-Western drawl or two from across the Atlantic and the accents of Middle England, chunky Yorkshire and grey estuary English… A babble, certainly, but at least as far as the English goes, very little that you cannot understand.

Previous page:
The Gothic fluting of the roof of Canterbury Cathedral

Left: The undercroft at the Eastbridge Hospital of St Thomas the Martyr. Here pilgrims would have rested on straw mats after their journey to pay homage at St Thomas's shrine.

What would the medieval traveller have been listening to as he made his way up the Canterbury street towards the Cathedral? How did the English speak in Chaucer's time?

Melvyn Bragg asked **Dr Kathryn Lowe** of the University of Glasgow this question. They sat beneath the arched ceiling of the Undercroft of the Eastbridge Hospital of St Thomas the Martyr in Canterbury. The word 'hospital' originally meant a place where you could get hospitality, a hostel, and only later came to mean somewhere where you went for medical attention. This particular hospital was founded in 1198 to provide a resting place for weary pilgrims after their journey to the shrine of St Thomas à Becket. There, where the pilgrims would have slept or rested on their rush mats, **Dr Lowe** talked about the way people spoke in Chaucer's 1395:

The first point to make is that they would definitely have been speaking English. At that time, Canterbury pilgrims who came from the highest social class, as well as the lowest, might have spoken English, French or even, amazingly to us today, a form of Latin. By this period, I don't think anyone outside the Court would have been speaking French as a main language, but they might have used some phrases closely related to Latin. A medieval Melvyn Bragg, as a writer, would have had the same choice of three languages – Latin, French and, increasingly, English. English was gaining considerable ground as a written language at this period. Although, after the Norman Conquest, a great number of French words would have entered the language, English would have continued to be spoken by the vast majority of people. Quite clearly the Anglo-Normans had a big influence on vocabulary, but they didn't really affect the structure of the language, in the same way as the Norse settlers did. The sound of the Canterbury streets in Chaucer's time – the 1390s – would have been rather like walking through, say, Cambridge today where you hear other languages spoken almost more than English. Canterbury was a place of pilgrimage; a mixture of different accents and different dialects would have been heard in the streets around the Cathedral. Here you would have

heard spoken every dialect.

Oddly, Kentish, the speech here in Canterbury, seemed to be the particular butt of many jokes during the Middle English period. It was rather like, for example, the way some people sometimes make fun of the Birmingham accent today. During the later Middle English period, Kentish dialect was the one they really went for, and I think the reason for this is because Kent is quite close to London. People would have heard locals from Kent and have been familiar with how they spoke. Then again Kent had been the focus of a number of rebellions, like the Peasants' Revolt, for example, (when Wat Tyler led thousands of poor people to London in 1380 to protest against the taxes imposed on them to pay for the war with France) and Kent was therefore considered to be very working class, very 'peasanty'. Scholars have noted a number of writers at this time trying to imitate the Kentish accent and no doubt getting a whole series of cheap laughs from it, much as we might today from trying a stage Somerset accent!

People coming from different parts of the country would have had some considerable difficulty in understanding each other. We've got reasonably strong evidence about this. We see, in a fourteenth century text, somebody complaining that the people from the South can't understand the people from the North. And he has a special gripe against people from Yorkshire, saying in particular that they speak in such a sharp, piercing, formless fashion that it is almost impossible to understand them!

It's not just like somebody today with a broad Glaswegian accent being perhaps slightly hard to understand if you're from the South, or vice versa, because in the regional Englishes we're talking about in the fourteenth century, there's a whole series of dialect words for a start, a completely different vocabulary. And also there are differences in word endings as well (to denote different grammatical cases) just to complicate the issue even further. For example, the north of

Canterbury Cathedral

England, with a dialect derived from Northumbrian Anglo-Saxon, tended to have the third-person singular form of verbs in 's' (like '*he thinks*', just as today), whereas in Chaucer's (southern) language the ending would be in '– eth' – '*he thinketh*'. Eventually it is the northern form that is going to win. So these regional Englishes were proper dialects; not just accents, not just a matter of pronunciation.

Middle English, as it was spoken in Chaucer's time, was different from the Old English of King Alfred's time, chiefly because it had lost many of the inflectional endings of the older language. However, documentary evidence of the sort of English people were speaking is patchy. For a while, after the Normans arrived, it is difficult to trace. Latin and French take over as the language of literature and in legal and other documents. When, 150 years later, our evidence of how spoken English was faring re-emerges, it is naturally bound to look rather different because it has undergone a century and a half of evolution. There are signs, even within Old English, that the loss of inflectional endings, which we would consider to be a feature of Middle English, is already starting to take place.

An inflected language is one in which the job which a word does in a sentence is indicated by the sort of ending it has. In modern English we still have some traces of the old inflectional system today. For instance, we put an *s* on plural nouns: we distinguish between one dog and two dog*s*. This is inflection in its simplest form. In Old English, though, the inflection system was much more developed, so that people distinguished between the subject and the object of a sentence by using different endings, not simply by the word order they used. So you could say 'The man saw the lady' and it would be obvious, even if the word order of the two nouns were reversed in the sentence, that it was the man doing the seeing – not the lady – because man and lady would have different sorts of endings which would conform to a pattern. If it was the lady seeing the man

the Anglo-Saxon words would be *hlaefdige* and *guman*, but in the man saw the lady they would *guma* and *hlaefdigan*. During the Middle English period those endings tend to fall away and word-order takes over as the shaper of the sense of sentences. Nowadays the accepted order of subject – verb – object tells us immediately that it was the man seeing the lady. However the process was a gradual one that started many years before Geoffrey Chaucer's time.

Judging by the rhymes in Chaucer, the Middle English he spoke must have sounded rather different from our language. The main difference lies in the way vowels were pronounced. A big change occurred in pronunciation in late medieval times called the Great Vowel Shift. Why it happened is a matter of hot academic debate, but **Dr Lowe** explained why she believes it was probably a question of social climbing and snobbery:

The view I adhere to is that the Great Vowel Shift in the South might have been triggered by an attempt by some speakers to actually imitate upper class London pronunciation, to mimic the speech of people they looked up to, but they just overshoot that tiny little bit and they push into making major changes of pronunciation. For example, take a word like modern English 'name'. At Middle English times that vowel would have been pronounced as in the vowel *a* in 'father', "NAH-MUH". During the Great Vowel Shift, that's going to change to "EH", and then from there it's quite an easy step to the modern pronunciation of "NAYM"."

This process of shifting sounds to another position in the mouth affected a lot of vowels, including all the long vowels; all the vowels are raised and those that can't be raised are turned into diphthongs. Thus words like 'wife' and 'house', which in Chaucer's time were pronounced with the vowel sounds of modern English 'see' and 'zoo'. acquired the pronunciation we use today. The process was less noticeable in the North, but in the South and the Midlands it was very extensive indeed, such that after the Great Vowel Shift, English began to sound much more, though not

Translating Chaucer

Chaucer wrote in the sort of language which marked the transition of Middle English into modern English, so that although some of the words are immediately familiar, others are not. The first eight lines of 'The Prologue to the Canterbury Tales' look difficult, but once we have modernised the word order and grasped a few basic differences between Chaucer's language and our own it is less daunting:

> Whan that Aprille, with hise shoures soote,
> When April with its sweet showers
> The droghte of March hath perced to the roote
> has pierced the drought of March to the root
> And bathed euery veyne in swich licour
> and bathed every vein in such liquor
> Of which vertu engendred is the flour
> from which strength the flower is engendered
> Whan Zephirus eek with his sweete breeth
> When Zephirus also with his sweet breath
> Inspired hath in every holt and heeth
> has breathed upon in every woodland and heath
> The tendre croppes and the yonge sonne
> the tender shoots, and the young sun
> Hath in the Ram his half cours yronnne
> Has run his half course in the Ram

The conventions of literary language – the allusion to Zephyrus, the west wind – and to astrology – the sign of the ram– may be unfamiliar, but the actual vocabulary Chaucer uses here needs very little translation. It is the spelling which is different. Only a few hints are needed for a modern reader to be able to immediately translate.

The first point to notice is that in Chaucer's day words were very often spelt with a single vowel where we would use a double one – or vice versa. A word like *seke* has become seek, *slepe* has become sleep, *swete* has become sweet. Sometimes the vowels are slightly different, but not so different as to make *whan* or *breeth* or *bif* difficult to guess. The next point to notice is that many verbs and nouns have lost their endings. Plural verbs have an ending –en which does not exist in present day English, so we say make and long, rather than *maken* and *longen* or help instead of *holpen*. Verbs like *goon* or *yronne* have been simplified, losing the inflections which Middle English originally inherited from the Germanic languages. Instead of them, Chaucer uses *hem,* and nouns such as *sonne* or *croppe* have lost their endings. Some things, such as the use of *y* where we would use the letter *i* or *hath* instead of has, are more familiar.

Now translate the next lines of The Prologue. The four lines about small birds being pricked in their hearts (*corages*) and sleeping with open eyes are straightforward read. Perhaps the *palmeres who long to seek ferne halwes* (far off saints) may present a momentary problem, but after that you won't look back.

> And smale foweles maken melodye,
> That slepen al the nyght with open eye–
> So priketh hem Nature in hir corages–
> Thanne longen folk to goon on pilgrimages
> And palmeres for to seken straunge strondes
> To ferne halwes, kowthe in sondry londes;
> And specially, from every shires ende
> Of Engelond, to Caunturbury they wende,
> The hooly blisful martir for to seke
> That hem hath holpen, whan that they were seeke
> Bifil that in that seson, on a day,
> In Southwerk at the Tabard as I lay,
> Redy to wenden on my pilgrymage
> To Caunterbury, with ful devout corage,
> At nyght were come into that hostelrye
> Wel nyne and twenty in a compaignye

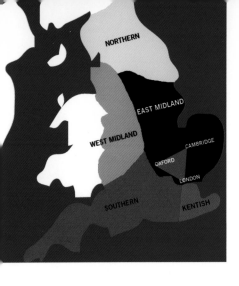

A map showing the areas where the different dialects were spoken at the time of Chaucer.

entirely, like our present day language.

The English we read in *The Prologue to the Canterbury Tales*, quoted above, was essentially the same as the English which was generally spoken in Chaucer's time. Chaucer was, of course, writing a piece of literature so the vocabulary might have been rather different – the sort of words we use when we speak every day are obviously not necessarily the same as those we might choose to write in a major piece of verse. Then there would be differences depending on where people came from. If they were Northerners, from Cumbria, say, like Melvyn Bragg, their English would have been different from someone like Chaucer, whose own dialect was essentially that of the central to east Midlands. Overall, however, Chaucer's English is quite a good guide to the way people from the southern counties of England spoke in the late fourteenth century.

Modern English turned out to be a mixture of the different regional dialects, but by far the most influential was that of the East Midlands, chiefly because it was the largest area (see the map on this page) and had the highest population. It also covered London, Oxford and Cambridge, so it embraced the most important centres of learning, political administration, social life and the law. It was strategically situated between the northern and southern regions, providing a useful bridge between them, and it was a rich agricultural area, fast developing a lucrative wool trade. Important trading links were being established with the Continent, which were to provide much of the country's wealth for several generations. This was definitely the place to be if you were looking for social position and prestige. The East Midlands dialect was the dialect of power.

Dr. **Ruth Evans** of Cardiff University, who joined Melvyn Bragg and Dr Lowe in Canterbury, felt we should be wary of using Chaucer's work as a representation of spoken Middle English. He is not, according to **Dr. Evans**, offering a sort of transcription of real life:

It's significant that he does give an illusion of freshness and a kind of directness, yet it is

73

The Shrine of St Thomas à Becket in Canterbury Cathederal. The swords overhead are a reminder of the way he was stabbed to death by Knights who thought they were doing the will of Henry II.

nevertheless an illusion. *The Wife of Bath's Prologue*, for instance, is an absolute tour de force of dramatic performance, really drawing the audience in and giving them a sense of a spoken voice. That's what modern readers feel when they hear *The Prologue* read out aloud – or even when they are reading it to themselves; the use of language creates that sense of a living, speaking being. What Chaucer is doing here, particularly in *The Wife of Bath's Prologue,* is let the reader be seduced by her language because he wants to make a point about the seductiveness of language itself.

In her very dramatic opening speech which begins:

> Experience, though noon auctoritee
> Were in this world, were right ynogh to me
> To speke of wo that is in mariage....

What she is doing is pitting experience, the experience of having been married to 5 husbands, against *auctoritee* or authority. *Auctoritee* is the authority of the Church. She is contrasting theory and practice, saying 'forget what the books say, I'm actually going to give it to you from the horse's mouth', and that

Thomas à Becket

In the Middle Ages Canterbury was one of the holy towns of England. Pilgrims travelled from all over Europe to pay homage at the shrine of St Thomas à Becket, the 'blisful holy martyr'. Thomas had been a close friend of King Henry II until Henry decided to make him the Archbishop of Canterbury, the head of the Church in England. In this position he had to defend the Church against the power of the State. This brought him into conflict with the King who wanted to make certain changes in the way in which the law courts worked, particularly the ecclesiastical courts. Thomas objected to this, threatening to excommunicate many of the King's supporters and close the churches. One day in December 1170, Henry flew into a rage and was heard to complain that none of his knights did anything to protect him from this tiresome Archbishop. Hearing this, four knights rushed over to Canterbury and murdered Thomas in his own cathedral. Henry is said to have been overcome with grief and to have worn a hair shirt for the rest of his life. Becket himself was immediately revered as a martyr. He was buried in the Cathedral and his shrine soon became a shrine at which miracles occurred. In 1174 he was canonised by the Pope and the shrine, containing his relics, became a focal point for pious pilgrims.

makes what she's saying very powerful, because the sense of realism contributes to the drama. The reader recognises each character as an individual, through his or her choice of subject and manner of telling the respective tales; and behind that hears the voice of Chaucer, who is presenting all the characters and their tales. The Wife of Bath's language is actually very mixed, in that she is drawing on and exploiting clerical language which she manages to pepper with colloquialisms. She becomes the embodiment of what she is saying.

Other stylistic devices Chaucer uses in order to give the text life like vitality include the use of asides and speaking directly to the audience, where pilgrims turn to other pilgrims and address them giving a sense of interaction, of the atmosphere of a party. In this way Chaucer gives a broad picture of the sort of sentiments particular types of people might have and the different ways they express them. However, although we do get some sense of the state of spoken English at this time, it is important to remember that he is engaged in a work of literature, imagining and shaping the way people speak, rather than recording what he hears.

Dr Evans went on to talk about Harry Baily, the innkeeper – the Host – of the Tabard Inn from which the pilgrims of *The Canterbury Tales* set out. He speaks with a great immediacy and vitality that suggests the freshness of real speech. He is a Common Man figure who is often used in *the Tales* to represent a medieval version of the-man-on-the-Clapham-omnibus's response to what's going on. In *The Pardoner's Tale* Harry Baily gets beside himself with anger when he thinks the Pardoner is displaying hypocrisy. Pardoners in the Middle Ages sold relics and were known to be corrupt. Having just told a moralising tale, and having been quite open with his audience that he is himself not a moral person, he nevertheless asks them to buy his pigs' bones which are masquerading as holy relics. The host gets furious at this and says '*I would I had thy coylans in my hand. I would they were enshrined in an hogges turd.*' In translation, this means I wish I had thy *coylans* – thy balls – in my hand and I would like them to be shrined in a hog's turd'. **Dr Evans** observes:

There is a nice mixture there of the word *coylans* which is French or Anglo-Norman, and which might have reminded some of Chaucer's listeners of a very famous passage in the French classic work of courtly love, *Le Roman de la Rose* (*the Romance of the Rose*). Turd, on the other hand, is most definitely a down-to-earth native English word. French influence had permeated English in all registers, and French words were found in the speech of rough and uneducated people as well as the aristocracy.

In *The Reeve's Tale*, Chaucer brings great vividness to his text – and a sense of the spoken language – by using northern dialect. Alan and John, the Clerks or students, come from the north of England village of Strother, which was so far north that the London audience couldn't be expected to know about it. Into their mouths Chaucer puts northern dialect terms like *wanges* for cheeks ('*...the wanges in his heed"*) and *heythen* for '*hence*' ('*pray yow spede us heythen...'*).

It's very interesting, said Dr Lowe, he doesn't overplay his hand there. He could have used far more forms reminiscent of the North, but Chaucer tones it down a little. It's been suggested that it may have been because he wanted his audience still to understand these two students and what they were saying. Later scribes copying his manuscript – this was still, of course, the pre-Caxton, pre-printing era – seem not to have understood this subtlety . They tried to help Chaucer out by adding a few more northern touches here and there!

Dr Evans draws distinctions with other works of the same period such as William Langland's *Piers Plowman* and *Sir Gawain and the Green Knight*. Langland is a much more urgent voice; he's trying to galvanise people into action. He is much more concerned with social injustice than Chaucer. *Gawain* contains a number of dialect words, written, as it was, by a poet from the Midlands or north of England, from Staffordshire or maybe Lancashire. Dialect words that might not have been

Chaucer's contemporaries

William Langland wrote *Piers Plowman* , a long poem
in Middle English, in about 1367-70. Although it has
great imaginative power, it is a rambling and
sometimes confusing work, consisting of four visions
in which the narrator introduces various allegorical
figures such as the Seven Deadly Sins on the one
hand and Charity and Conscience on the other.
During the course of these visions Langland manages
to explore various aspects of truth, life and religious
duty, exalting the simple life of the ordinary, hard
working peasant and satirising the corrupt practices of
the clergy.

John Gower (?1330-1408) was a friend of Chaucer
and one of the people to whom Chaucer dedicated his
poem '*Troilus and Criseyde*'. He was a very learned
man who wrote poetry in three languages – Latin,
French and English – and on a range of subjects.
Perhaps his best known work is the *Confessio
Amantis*, published in 1390, which draws on a wide
variety of classical stories and medieval romances to
present philosophical and moral themes.

'*Sir Gawain and the Green Knight*' is an alliterative
poem based on the idea of King Arthur and his Court
and embodying all the ideals of medieval chivalry.
Ideals of faith, honour and loyalty are tested and only
very slightly betrayed, so that everyone ends up
rejoicing together in knightly duty. It is generally
considered to be one of the greatest poems in Middle
English but very little is known of its origin, except that
it probably came from the north west Midlands and
dates from the second half of the fourteenth century.

Marjery Kempe (c1373-1439) was a mystic who
travelled on pilgrimages to the great medieval shrines
at places like Rome, Compostella, Jerusalem and
Wilsnack in Poland. In her '*Book of Marjery Kempe*'
she recounts stories of her travels, her experience of
life and her religious visions.

understood by an audience in the south
England were deliberately used, bein
deliberately exploited by the Gawain po
because he wants to show up difference
between the conventions of French Romanc
and the immediacy of English Romance, an
what English vernacular poets can do with th
verse forms.

It's true, adds Dr Lowe, **that Chaucer's wo
has enjoyed a really pre-eminent positio
amongst medieval literature. There are tw
good reasons for this. Firstly, he's a crackin
good poet who, secondly, is writing in
language which is not very far removed fro
that standard language which was going t
become our present day English. There ar
many small vernacular touches in the wor
such as, in *The Miller's Tale*, when th
character of Alison, playing a filthy practic
joke on Absalom, shuts a window in his fac
and exclaims 'tee-hee'. ('He ...seyde, fy
allas! what have I do? Tehee! quod she, an
clapte the wyndow to...') You can actuall
engage with that on a level where yo**

possibly can't engage so much with more pedestrian poets like Langland who's full of good moral sentiments – good for you – but not so much fun.

There is an element of accident about the fact that Chaucer gained such pre-eminent stature from his writing in a dialect which was, while not exactly the dialect that became standard English, close enough for it to give it a particular currency. It's important not to be dogmatic about Chaucer as a kind of colossus striding the fourteenth century and to remember other writers of the time who are contributing to the sense of the language as a living medium. East Anglian writers, for instance, like Marjery Kempe were writing in the early fifteenth century. Their language, and, indeed their works, were of real stature, but weren't written in a dialect which subsequently becomes that of present day spoken English.

The medieval audience for *The Canterbury Tales* would most likely have heard the words spoken aloud. Literacy was limited, so reading a book, for most people, meant hearing it. This was true, even of the – largely courtly – audience for which Chaucer would principally have been writing. Right up to the fifteenth century, people often preferred to hear text read aloud than to read it silently themselves.. There is evidence, from fifteenth century books of royal households, that sitting listening to chronicles read aloud was a 'recreational pursuit' for an evening. People would also share opinions about what they were reading with others in a collaborative manner which perhaps today's notion of private study has taken us away from. During the medieval period there was virtually no such phenomenon as 'silent' reading. If you went into a monastery, it was a very noisy place because people were busy reading aloud, even if they were reading to themselves. It was a hubbub of excitement. In a library no one would be turning around going 'shush'!

Dr Lowe talked about the relationship between speech and writing:

When you actually look at the vast numbers of manuscripts surviving from the late medieval period it is important to realise that Middle English literature is not just Chaucer, it's not even just Chaucer and Langland and the Gawain poet. There's a whole body of other material – non literary texts, minor poems, some lyrics and a load of prose. In those we can actually spot dialects that work. It's always very hard to interpret the difference between stuff which is written down and how that actually would have sounded. For instance, there are over 500 different recorded ways of spelling the word 'through' in late middle English. That's just recorded ways – goodness knows how many others there were that haven't been recorded. Other people whose works haven't survived might have spelt it differently. One is d.o.r.w.g.h. What are we to make of that? Another one is þ.o.w.r.w. (þ is the Old English letter called 'thorn' and pronounced 'th') How are we going to interpret that in terms of accent? That is a different and a difficult problem because it is going to be quite hard to make that relationship between speech and writing. We've constantly got to remember that what we are seeing is actually written on the manuscripts and the way people write things down has just as much effect on the language as the way they actually speak themselves.

The introduction of the printing press by William Caxton, some eighty years after Chaucer wrote *The Canterbury Tales*, made a huge impact on the way English looked on the page. For the written language, printing encouraged standardisation. Before printing, manuscripts would be copied all over the country in different dialects, with every possibility of transcribing errors at every stage of copying. But once a text is set in type and is printed, it becomes a standard copy to be spread across the country and linguistic variety is diminished.

Dr Lowe talked about this change:

Although spoken English is not going to be standardised for many more centuries, I think the standardisation that printing brought to the written word had something to add to the process

Pilgrimages

Pilgrimages were an important part of Christian life in Chaucer's time. People of all classes would go on them and they would often develop into a great party or holiday for the people involved. Really adventurous pilgrims might set out for the shrine of St James of Compostello in Spain or other continental holy shrines, making it an excuse for a tour of the Continent to broaden their experience. It was seen as a once in a lifetime opportunity. Even for pilgrims like Chaucer's, travelling to Canterbury, it was a chance to meet new people, to mix with or at least to observe people of different social classes and to hear news from other parts of the country.

However, the main reason why people went on the journey was to pay homage to St. Thomas. Sometimes they went to thank him for having interceded with God on their behalf when they were in a tight spot, or to try and make sure of his help in the future. Sometimes they went as an act of penitence, having been told by the priest that a pilgrimage would bring them redemption and make it easier for them to avoid the horrors of hell. The journey from London to Canterbury would take several days, depending on the speed at which the pilgrims wanted to travel. Usually they would go on horseback, but sometimes, as an extra penance, they would go on foot or deliberately find a way of making the journey uncomfortable for themselves in the hope that the extra hardship would make doubly sure of the redemption.

The journey itself would be festive rather than gloomy. Intending pilgrims would probably stay a night at an inn on the south side of London before setting off. Then in the morning, everyone who was ready to go would simply form a group and set off together. They would stop overnight at one of the 'hostelries' known as convenient stopping places for pilgrims where many of them would just join a large room full of people sleeping on mats on the floor.

Obviously, such a popular tourist route would attract people who had something to sell. It was a good opportunity for clergy to set up stalls selling religious ornaments, 'relics' or 'pardons'. Souvenirs of the saint, mass produced from moulds were sold in their thousands. The gathering of pilgrims was also a good opportunity to preach the gospel and reinforce the doctrines of the Church, so it was in the Church's interest to insist that pilgrimage was necessary for the salvation of the soul.

of standardisation within spoken English too. It had, I think, the effect of marginalising certain accents and certain dialects because readers of written texts were now seeing a standard English originating from another local variety and that's going to marginalise other dialects.

Chaucer wrote in a language which is not very far removed from that standard language which was going to become our present day English. It's no accident, therefore, that he's a school text man. People sitting A levels will read Chaucer but they would never be able to read '*Gawain and the Green Knight*', which was written round about the same time, because it is written in a dialect which is completely removed from our standard English. It, therefore, takes a hefty index to be able to understand it. You've got to know something about the language to be able to really engage with that poem. Interestingly, Chaucer is enjoyed today and has always been enjoyed through the centuries, often for different reasons. He has managed to retain that sort of pre-eminent position because different generations have enjoyed different things about him.

Finally, a comment from **Terry Jones**, the writer and humorist, who has been writing about Chaucer and agreed to be interviewed:

It was very significant that Chaucer wrote in English. If he had wanted to get on in the world he would have done what his friend Gower did, he would have written one poem in Latin, one poem in French and one poem in English. He was perfectly capable of writing in those languages and, in fact, he may have written some poems in French, but he wanted to write in English because he wanted to communicate with the poor ploughman, the parson and the people who didn't have Latin and didn't have these other languages, who didn't have the privileges of a Court or clerical background. He wanted to empower these people, who were outside the Court and the Church with knowledge and to bring the world of learning to ordinary people. He was not alone in doing that. It was all part of that egalitarian feel which was very important in that period.

EDIN

BURGH

5

Edinburgh, the capital of Scotland and now home to the Scottish Parliament is, when the sun shines, one of the most blessed cities in Europe. Wide crescents and spacious terrace houses set aside the austerity of their stone façades to glow in the full splendour of summer.

August in Edinburgh is International Festival time. For a fortnight it is the capital of the arts world. Princes Street, the majestic central boulevard, with its grand shops to one side and the Castle crenellating the opposite horizon, is thronged with festival-goers. The accents on Princes Street on a summer day are cosmopolitan, as likely to be American-English, Spanish, French or German as they are Scots or even Anglo-English. Edinburgh is, at this moment more than any other, a city of international inclination. Yet across the centuries, across the shifts of power and influence in religion, politics and fashion, Edinburgh has always shown an open face to the world beyond these islands.

The 'auld alliance' with France may have been largely a defensive gesture against England but it also served to give Scottish culture an extra dimension. And Scots faces were again turned to look far overseas when, in the nineteenth century, the Highland clearances forced thousands from their territorial lands in the north and west of Scotland and into emigrant exile abroad. Their descendants return in their numbers to the old country, bringing new ways of speaking, mingling their different cultures and making Edinburgh an international city.

The histories of England and Scotland have long been wound together in rivalry and pride. In 1603 King James VI of Scotland also became King James I of England, thus uniting the two monarchies. Just over a hundred years later, in 1707, the Treaty of Union confirmed that joint sovereignty. But governance and sovereignty are complex affairs and the power-relationships that have both connected and divided London and Edinburgh, over the thousand years we are looking at in this book (1000 – 2000), are bound up inextricably with matters of religion and belief.

At the heart of the period from 1474 –1707, which we focus on in this chapter, is the effect of the Reformation and Henry VIII's split with the Church of Rome. In breaking away from Rome, England also broke its allegiance to Latin which was the Catholic Church's language of expression. Now English, the language of Protestantism, took over as the preferred medium of theology as well as government, though it still had a battle to fight with Latin during the Renaissance, when it came to the articulation of scientific ideas. In Scotland, the Reformation's most powerful voice of Protestantism was the Edinburgh preacher, John Knox. He stood in bitter theological and cultural opposition to Mary Queen of Scots (daughter of Scotland's King James V and his French wife Mary of Guise) who was seen as a Catholic figurehead. They are both symbols of their time and of the power struggle that was going on. Their lives, their perceptions of their role in life and their ways of expressing it, illustrate the characteristics of that struggle.

The period of 200 or so years following the birth of printing is known to linguists as the age of Early Modern English. In Scotland during this time, the language of popular expression is a form of English, formally known as Scots. This is a language that draws strength from Norse and French sources as well as its bedrock status as a national variety of English. It is far removed from the Celtic language of the islands known as Gaelic, and has a linguistic evolution all its own which is parallel with, but distinct from, the English of the English Midlands. As we saw in the previous chapter, by the time of Caxton's introduction of the printing-press, a much more standardised form of English was emerging. Over the next two and a quarter centuries that would develop into a form of English which differs very little in shape and sound from the language of today.

UNTO ME IS THIS GRACE GIVEN THAT I SHOULD PREACH THE UNSEARCHABLE RICHES OF CHRIST

To explore the evolution of Early Modern English and the rise of its power over French and Latin, as well as its parallel and distinct close-cousin, Scots, Melvyn Bragg talked to Dr Kathryn Lowe of Glasgow University and J Derrick McClure of Aberdeen University. They met in the house of John Knox which, in the sixteenth century, was the headquarters of the Reformation in Scotland.

The John Knox House stands about halfway down the Royal Mile between Edinburgh Castle and Holyrood Palace. It is a narrow, tall building with stone steps leading into small beamed rooms, many of the beams decorated in the typical Scottish style of the time, with looping coloured line patterns. On the walls there are blown up printed extracts from the sermons of the great Reformation preacher and his disciples: 'I assure you the voice of this one man John Knox is able in one hour to put more life in us than five hundred trumpets continually blasting in our ear' reads one quotation. 'A Scot', in the words of Melvyn Bragg, 'who used English to preach the doctrines of Protestantism, thundering his addresses to the crowd from the room in which I'm sitting'. The story of Early Modern English is both a tale of language in the time of Knox and a landmark in religious literature. The Authorised King James version of the Bible shows what the English language is capable of. It also shows the power which English found itself developing during the Renaissance. This was a language now called upon to organise ideas, to describe new concepts and to create vast structures of the imagination, at a time of exploration and discovery both in science and the arts. And it is, of course, the age of that most powerful manipulator of the English language, William Shakespeare.

t is a time when the notion of the modern nation state is being clarified and English is now elaborated and expanded, as it is called on to do a national job rather than a local or a regional one, in parliament, in church, in science and the arts. An English – or Scots – man or woman is now defined in terms of the language he or she speaks.

At the point in the development of English at which this chapter begins, the people of Edinburgh would have been speaking a language known as Scots. It was the language of the mass of the Scottish people.

Scots, explains Derrick McClure, **like modern English, has its roots in Old English, but while English originates from a Midlands dialect, Scots is descended from a northern variety of Anglo-Saxon or Old English. It is a language which has always been closely related to English and which belongs to the same family. It has no connection with the other indigenous tongue of Scotland, Gaelic.**

Gaelic belongs to a completely different language family. It is a community language now spoken only in the far west of Scotland and in substantial 'colonies' of immigrant Gaelic speakers in the cities, especially Glasgow. But it was at one time spoken over a wide area right into the central hinterland and down into the South West as well. Scots and English are more or less mutually comprehensible and even when there are differences, there are regular correspondences: where English has words like *home* and *stone*, in Scots it's *hame* and *stane*. Where the English say *town* and *down* in Scots it's *toon* and *doon*. The English *moon* and *good* in Scots correspond to *muin* and *guid*. But the differences are not merely ones of pronunciation: the vocabulary of Scots is very distinctive. The ten volume Scottish National Dictionary, which includes all the words that are unique and distinctive to Scots, lists more than 70,000 entries.

Unsurprisingly, Scots has borrowed words from Gaelic – like *ingle* for fireplace, but also from Scandinavian languages as well as from Dutch and French. English, however, has taken a different path. If you look at the poet, Robert Burns, you'll find *cranreuch*, which is a word for

The house in Edinburgh where John Knox lived, and which is now a Museum. He is believed to have preached from an upstairs window, declaiming to the people down in the street.

rost, or *messan* which is a word for a small dog. They're from Gaelic. Or a word like *bucht* which means both a sheep pen, and a boxed in pew in a church: that's a Dutch borrowing. French gives you *ashet* for example, a flat plate, or *tass*, a cup, – or tassie as it very often is. Gaelic gives you *quaich* which is another kind of cup, another kind of drinking vessel. The Scandinavian influence gives you *kirk*, corresponding to church, and *brig* corresponding to bridge. You've got earned Latin, too, school-book Latin. This gives you *dominie* for teacher, or *pandie* for a smack n the hand with a *tawse*, or *fooge* for playing truant from school. So the vocabulary of Scots is very distinctive.

Furthermore, Scots has preserved words that used to belong to English, like *bide* for example, meaning stay, or *thole* meaning endure, which you find in Chaucer's English. They disappeared from standard literary English but survived in Scots. Scotland as an independent nation had close political and diplomatic relations with France and with the Netherlands, and so Scots wa[s] influenced by French and Dutch to an extent that English was not. At the same time, becaus[e] Gaelic was spoken in the same country, Scots borrowed quite a number of words from Gaelic not as many as you might think, but certainly some. With the departure of King James [to] London, the ruling classes, most of whom belonged to the Scottish aristocracy, went south wit[h] the court and developed the habit of spending part of the year in England, part of the year [in] Scotland. Thus they became bilingual: in England they learned to speak English, but on the return to Scotland, talking with their tenants and their dependents, they would talk Scots. S[o] at the time of King James, for the ruling, educated, literate, classes at least, reading an[d] speaking English as well as Scots presented few problems. But there was no suggestion tha[t] they should adopt English in place of Scots and still less that they should force their tenan[ts] and their dependents to do so. Scots continued as the language of the mass of the people. Th[e] main period of the Renaissance in the fifteenth and sixteenth and very early seventeent[h] centuries, was the richest period in the history of the Scots language. At this time Scotland wa[s] an independent kingdom within the British Isles and an independent power in Europe unde[r] very dynamic and flamboyant kings like James IV and V. They were determined to make [a] splash in Europe, to demonstrate to the courts of Europe that Scotland was a political an[d] military and cultural power to be reckoned with in Europe.

eneva Bible was compiled and published by a
·gation of English Protestant exiles, with the
h Reformer John Knox as their minister, in Calvin's
city of Geneva. It was the most complete and most
ite English translation of the Bible yet to have
red, and became the most widely-used English
until the Authorised King James Bible of 1611.
tland, the adoption of the Geneva Bible by the
nation Parliament of 1560 had the unintended
of enhancing the status of English at the expense
native Scots tongue.

At this time, there was a deliberate policy by the Kings of Scotland to encourage the arts –
literature and music in particular. The great poets of the period, Henryson and Dunbar, who
wrote in Scots, were certainly then among the finest writing in Europe. Earlier masters of
poetry in Scots, like Blind Harry in the reign of James III, or before him John Barbour under
Robert II, had deliberately written epics on Scottish national heroes such as Robert Bruce and
William Wallace. They depicted in verse form Scotland's success in the War of Independence
on the model of French romances and French historical or quasi-historical poems.

t was the Reformation and the adoption of the English version of the Bible in Scotland that
brought about the first reverses for the Scots language. You had the decree that every
household above a certain income level had to own a copy of the so-called 'Geneva Bible' which
was translated into English. It was common practice to read aloud and to preach from the
Bible, and so Scots people would be accustomed to hearing the scriptures read in English. The
ministers who read it would, of course, be Scotsmen and they would read it with their native
accents and their native pronunciation, but essentially in Scotland we got accustomed in the
time of the Reformation to hearing English, and associating English with the word of God –
which of course gave it a tremendous prestige.

Furthermore, as a result of the Reformation, the traditional Scottish connection with catholic
France was broken, and replaced by a very close spiritual connection with England. The fact,
too, that the descendants of Henry VIII were all childless made it likely that the Scottish
monarch was going to inherit the throne of England. **Derrick McClure** goes on to say:

This very close political connection between Scotland and England was foreseen well before it
happened, to prepare for which many members of the Scottish ruling classes began to think it
a good idea to start learning English and practise making use of it.

This is the printed text of a doctrinal argument in 1562 between John Knox and Quintyne, the Cat Abbot of Crosraguel (pronounced 'cross-REgal') in Ayrshire. It is of interest to note that whereas the At contributions are in almost unmixed Scots (*Monunday the sevint* for Monday the seventh, *heides* for h *na* for no, *or ye war* for before ye were, the peculiar use of the plural, found only in legal language, i *saides artickles*, and many other examples). Knox's language is rather more Anglicised (such inste *sic*, fewer then (i.e. 'than') instead of *fewer nor*. Knox's Anglicised speech was used as a debating po his Catholic oppor

Starting with the Reformation, about the time of James VI, metropolitan English was beginnin to supersede Scots. Scots had its high water mark in the early Stewart period when it ha become the official national language and the vehicle for one of the greatest vernacula literatures of Europe. Gradually, over the sixteenth and seventeenth centuries, it wa superseded by English as a medium of literary expression, although it remained the spoken lar guage among the majority of the Scottish people.

But the relationship was always ambiguous. In the medieval period, the great poets of Scot like Henryson and Dunbar and even the ardent patriotic poets, John Barbour and Blind Harr seemed to have felt no hostility at all to English as a cultural force. In fact, they certainl regarded Chaucer, Gower and Lydgate, as their masters and their models, and they considere themselves to be writing in the same tradition as these great English writers. So although the language was different, culturally there was no hostility corresponding to the very real politica hostility that there was between the Scottish and the English monarchies.

The linguistic watershed between Scots and English was the King James Bible, the so-calle 'Authorised Version', of 1611. This new translation, published under the authority of Kin James, monarch of the newly united Kingdoms of England and Scotland, was to mark one c the most significant moments in the establishment of a standardised and expressive shape f the national language of Britain.

It's interesting, comments Dr Kathryn Lowe, **how such a translation of the Bible was set i motion. King James was actually on his way down from Scotland to London and was presente with a petition demanding a new translation of the Bible. The petitioners expresse dissatisfaction with existing versions thinking that King James would be in sympathy with the puritan beliefs. Obviously they were wrong in that, but King James wanted a kind of litera**

the abbotes second

letter, whereunto anſwer is made brieflie
to euerie head of the ſame.

M. Quintyne.

Ohn knox I reſſaued zour writing,
this monūday the ſeuint of Septem-
ber, and conſidered the heides thairof,
and firſt quhair ze ſay, zour cūming
in this cuntrie, was not to ſeik diſputation, but
ſimple to propone vnto the people, Jeſus Chriſt
crucified, to be the onely Sauiour of the warld,
praiſe be to God, that was na newingis in this
cuntrie, or ze war borne.

John Knox.

I greatlie dout, if euer Chriſt Jeſus wes treu-
lie preached, by a papiſticall prelat or monk.

M. Quintyne.

Secondlie, quhair ze alledge that I proclamed
in oppen audience blaſphemous artickles (he is
ane euil iudge that condemnis or he knawes)
than had bene tyme to zow to haif called them
blaſphemous, quhen ze had ſene them, red them,
and ſufficientlie confutated them.

John Knox.

I had hard them, and thereof I feared not to
pronunce them ſuche as they are.

M. Quintyne.

Thridly, quhair ze alledge that I promiſt decla-
ration of the ſaides artickles, on Sonday laſt
was,

heritage, he wanted to have been responsible for something himself, and so the King James Bible was begun.

The Bible in English continued to be a powerful motor for the spread of the English language within Scotland. **Derrick McClure** points out that there were various translations available: the Authorised Version and before it, the Geneva Bible, were but two.

With the Reformation, came the practice of using vernacular versions of the scriptures. With the publication of the magnificent Authorised Version, one of the finest monuments in the history of the English language, the Bible was used not only in the churches but in the schools – children learned to read and write by copying bits of it out. People knew great swathes of the Bible from a very early age, learning the psalms and many passages from the Gospels and the Epistles by heart. As the Bible text was in English, these young Scottish schoolchildren had to recite them in English – maybe painfully and with their native Scottish accents – but nonetheless in English.

Even though he was writing at the height of the greatest flowering of Scots culture, John Knox composed his *Historie of the Reformation* in English, not in the language of the Edinburgh where his house stands to this day. In fact, his great work is an inconsistent mixture of English and Scots.

Knox had spent part of his life in England as Chaplain to Edward VI and another period of his life ministering to congregations of English exiles and refugees in Switzerland. Thus, having spent a lot of his life among English-speaking people, his spoken language was probably English, though articulated with a Scottish accent. He came back from his exile at one point to preach in Ayr, and was taken for an Englishman; though very probably when he came back to Scotland permanently his language became much more Scotticised. He would have reverted to his roots

s for his writings, Knox was a bit of a hybrid, falling at times under the influence of both Scots and English linguistic traditions – just as he had in his life. So some of his letters are in almost pure Scots, while other correspondence with English friends and associates is in almost pure English. His magnum opus, the *Historie of the Reformation*, is written in a quite random, inconsistent mixture of the two. It is very interesting from a philological point of view to look at his *Historie* and see how sometimes he seems to have a Scots pronunciation in mind, but to write a word with an English spelling, or vice versa. Sometimes he'll use the Scots and the English equivalents for the same word almost within the space of the same page.

The period between the introduction of printing and the Treaty of Union, a span of a little more than two hundred years, sees English forging ahead, expanding and developing in a way that became unstoppable. The world was expanding – the great journeys to the New World and the East, the ferment of science and art throughout Europe, often under the opulent patronage of powerful regional baronies, produced an unparalleled requirement for a language which could describe those achievements. At the same time, the sound of English is still in the process of changing. The so-called Great Vowel Shift – the gradual and seemingly systematic movement around the mouth of the way English vowel sounds were made – was about to arrive at a more stable outcome. As the period comes to an end, the changes to the sound of English are less in the quality of individual vowels than in the stress patterns within the word. The word *balcony*, for instance, which was imported from Italy at this time, was pronounced with the emphasis on the '*o*' sound.

I think what you'd be surprised about, observes Dr Kathryn Lowe, **are the number of people who actually speak with a specific regional accent and still use dialect. The scientist, Isaac Newton, for example, showed great interest in phonetics – the study of the sounds of language – and**

even published some rough and ready transcriptions. These appear to reveal that he had a exceedingly strong Lincolnshire accent. Similarly, Richard Mulcaster, a writer and teacher wh commented on the large number of foreign words borrowed daily by the English languag 'either of pure necessities in new matters or of mere braverie, to garnish it self withal' had strong interest in spelling reform, but he apparently spoke with a strong northern accent.

What I'm particularly interested in is the way in which people start to stigmatise non-standa accents during this period. The school's inspectors at Richard Mulcaster's school complaine that the children were not being taught to pronounce their vowels correctly because there we so many northerners in the institution. That's very interesting, because although we' previously seen a form of stigmatisation of written English, we haven't really seen it in spoke English, and that is going to become more and more apparent. Henceforth there is a wide observed desire to speak 'correctly' and by the eighteenth century, there are a number text-books available whose object it is to teach readers to use grammar correctly.

However, as far as the actual sound of English was concerned, from about 1600 onwards you be able to understand people far more easily than would have been possible two hundred yea previously. English is now really going to take a new direction, augmenting its vocabulary in way which hadn't happened before and hasn't happened since. Thus, by the end of this perio English is going to be a self-confident language and able to express anything.

It is believed that in those two hundred years between 1500 and 1700 about 30,000 ne words were borrowed and became part of the language – more than any other time before since. Ironically, its users are not quite so self-confident, and, even as late as the eighteen century, they still worry about writing in English – as opposed to Latin which was the tradition mode of scholarly expression.

It was a time when people really started to worry about the way in which they were using their language as a factor that would mark them out socially. This was something quite new.

Although many of these new words were borrowed from Latin and Greek, in order to compensate' for what was felt to be the inadequacies of the English language, the trend is towards scholarly expression in the vernacular rather than in the traditional Latin. By about 1700, Newton was writing his *Opticks* in English, whereas his *Principia,* from just a few decades earlier, was printed in Latin.

Latin was the source of probably the greatest number of borrowings during this Renaissance expansion of English, providing words like *accommodate*, *industrial*, *absurdity*, *dexterity*, *adapt*, *alienate*, *illusion*, *assassinate*. Once the words have been borrowed, they could, naturally, be modified to suit the syntactic structure of English, so suffixes could be added to produce, for example, *numerous* or *numerality*. Yet, new 'Latinisms' such as these – words that today we think nothing of – at the time were subject to enormous criticism. They were popularly known as 'Inkhorn Terms'; in other words, terms essentially coined by pedants.

Thomas Wilson ridiculed them in his *Arte of Rhetorique* (1553):

"An ynkehorne letter. Pondryng, expendyng, and revolutyng with my self your ingent affabilitee, and inagenious capacitee, for mundane affaires: I cannot but celebrate and extolle your magnificall dexteritee, above all other. For how could you have adepted such ilustrate prerogative, and dominicall superioritee, if the fecunditee of your ingenie had not been so fertile, & wounderfull pregnaunt. Now therfore beeyuing accersited, to such splendent renoume & dignitee splendidious: I doubt not but you will adiuuate amiliaritee in Lincolneshire. Emong whom I beeyng a Scholasticall companion, obtestate your sublimitee to extoll myne infirmitee... Now whereas words be received, as well Greke as Latine, to set furthe our meanying in the englische tongue, either for lacke of store, or els because wee would enriche the language: it is well doen to use them, and no man therin can be charged for any affectacion, when all other are agreed to folowe the same waie... The folie is espied, when either we will use such words as fewe men doe use, or use theim out of place when another might serve muche better.

What's interesting, says Dr. Lowe, is the number of these words which we now use in everyday language, whereas other words, which also were laughed at then, have ceased to belong to either spoken or written languages. For example, to *deblaterate*, meaning to 'babble' has not survived, nor has the word to describe a dog barking – to *latrate*. Also if you were buried according to these Inkhorn terms that did not make the cut, you could be *consumulated*.

Say, for example, 'I baked you a cake' – well, I don't really like the word 'baked', it's rather .... rather English. So I use the word *pistated* – 'I have *pistated* you a cake', you see. And then, i my culinary skills aren't quite up to it, you might end up with a semi-*ustilated* cake, which is half-burnt cake. And if I were really no good at all in the kitchen, then you'd end up with

carbunculated cake – which is a cake which has been burnt to a cinder! And people actually used this exaggeratedly 'scholarly' vocabulary in order to sound that little bit more learned.

Our European neighbours, where the Renaissance flourished, brought rich cargoes of new vocabulary to the welcoming English. Fresh words had to be found for concepts that were new and needed description in terms where English was inadequate. There were new things that had to be wondered at, given names and consumed as exotica. From Italy came terms like 'balcony' and 'portico', reflecting knowledge of or interest in architecture. French too was still a major source of borrowings, although now the most useful vocabulary related very often to French exploration abroad. Words like 'chocolate' and 'moustache' join English via French during the Renaissance. Spanish and Portuguese exploration brought us words like 'apricot', 'banana', 'cocoa' – to describe new foodstuffs borne to our shores from faraway places. And, languages like French and Italian act as conduits, if you like, for languages from the Third World; so we see terms which are essentially, say, Indian in origin being borrowed first perhaps into Spanish, and then on, into English.

By the time of James VI of Scotland, however, the story of linguistic expansion in Scotland was essentially over. What **Derrick McClure** calls the 'glorious burgeoning and efflorescence' of Scots faded by the time of the great explorations when England was very much in the ascendant:

English was developing itself in the hands of great masters like Spenser and Shakespeare and now it was essentially English that held sway north ofthe border. By the late years of the reign of King James VI, a poet like Drummond of Hawthornden, who was a man of great learning and great intellectual curiosity, was writing pretty much in unmixed English, with very little to show from his writings that he was a Scotsman. Scotsmen were no longer able to express themselves to the same extent in the Scots language, but they now had the newly-expanded English at their disposal.

In eighteenth century Scotland, as in England, there was a very strong reaction against any language that was regarded as provincial or differed from the language spoken in London and at court. Unfortunately the educated classes in Scotland started thinking of their own language, their native Scots, as provincial and vulgar and improper. As a result, the misconception arose about it, (and it's a misconception that's still believed by many to this day), that Scots was a debased or corrupt or illiterate form of English.

Educated Scots now became very anxious, almost pathologically anxious, not to use any vocabulary or idioms that would mark them out as being Scottish. James Beattie, Professor of Greek at Aberdeen University, and the great philosopher, David Hume, drew up lists of 'Scotticisms', lists of Scots words and Scots idioms which they wanted their countrymen to avoid. They reveal quite a lot about the way Scots was spoken at the time. It was deemed inappropriate to say 'it was simply impossible', the correct expression being 'it was absolutely impossible'. Likewise, 'give me a drink' was proscribed in favour of 'give me some drink'. They were very fussy and very particular about anything they thought might possibly be regarded as Scottish, in order to keep their speech free from anything that could be taken as provincial or vulgar. But the odd thing is, this was never imposed by any Act of Parliament – it's not a case of the official ruling classes decreeing 'you're not to speak Scots you're to speak English'. This was something, and you can't speak of this without feeling uncomfortable and indeed ashamed, that the Scottish ruling classes, the leaders of opinion the leaders of literacy and culture in Scotland, started doing to themselves.

Scots – and Gaelic – still exist as spoken languages and are very much alive as literary languages. Scots, especially in the present century, has undergone a remarkable literary renaissance, and is still being used as a medium of expression for traditional poetry, for experimental poetry and for short stories.

Now, with the establishment in Edinburgh in 1999 of the Scottish Parliament, there is a hope amongst many Scots that, as well as Gaelic, which already has official recognition, the Parliamentarians will give official status to the Scots language. In the opinion of many, it should be given much greater recognition, with more attention paid to it in schools. **The hope is,** says Derrick McClure, **that the children who come from Scots-speaking households will not only be allowed but encouraged to use their native language in school, instead of being taught that it's something that they've got to be educated out of. It is, after all, the native tongue of the country.**

LIV

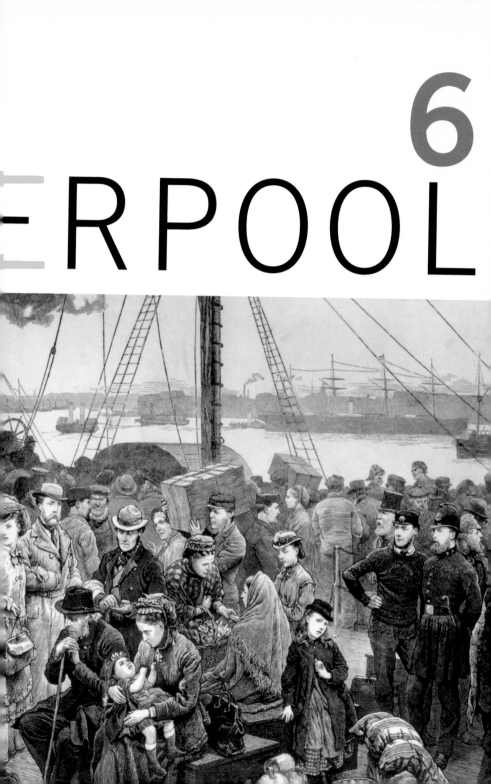

People waiting at the dock in Liverpool. They have either just arrived, perhaps from Ireland, or are waiting
depart. The picture suggests the mingling of styles, nationalities and cultures which brought about t
richness of Liverpool speech. It also illustrates the amount of activity on the River Mersey itse

Right: Liverpool, one of the centres of colonial trade with Africa, America and the West Indies, handled m
of the county's slave trade. This diagram shows the layout of a slave ship commonly known as a 'coffin sh
as they carried the sick, dying and often dead in the most appalling conditions. G.F. Cooke, a nineteer
century actor at the Theatre Royal Liverpool described the city as 'an infernal town, every brick of wh
was cemented with an African's blo

Liverpool. Great city, great port. A name that has for generations signified arrivals and departures. From Liverpool great liners like the *Mauretania* sailed on their record-breaking voyages across the Atlantic. To early eighteenth century Liverpool came, aboard the *Liverpool Merchant* and the *Blessing*, cargoes of cotton and sugar cane harvested in the West Indies by slaves from Africa. A century later, thousands of starving Irish followed, fleeing the famine across the Irish Sea.

Liverpool's skyline is legendary. The Liver Building, originally an insurance office block, breaking the skyline with its lumpy tower,now stands as a great civic symbol of reassurance and continuity. Across the city the neo-Gothic Anglican Cathedral squares up to its nineteen sixties' Catholic counterpart, symbols of the two religious and social traditions of a place where so many Irish Catholics have made their homes and enriched the city's speech with their accents.

So, Liverpool looks out welcomingly towards Ireland and on to America. It is a port to which ships have always come from all over the world, importing not only consumable goods and materials, but also all sorts of people with different ideas, different experiences and, most importantly, different languages. Some of them merely unloaded and loaded up again, ready to depart on another journey, but some, liking the look of Liverpool or having no immediate chance of another voyage, stayed and made their home there. They founded a community of their own and continued to speak their own language, but they also had to use English if they were going to flourish in this new environment, so they became bilingual, able to switch from one language to another according to the situation they were in. The two languages mingled and changed each other and the scope of English was increased.

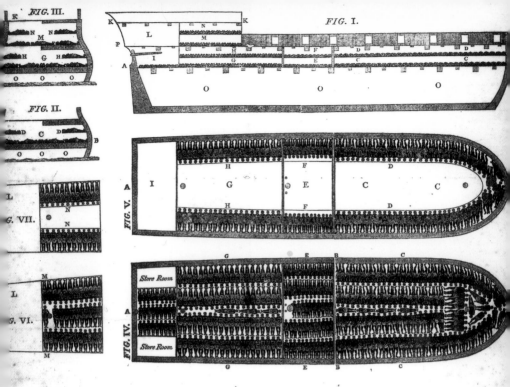

There are many distinct communities in this multiracial city. People have come from other countries to live here and have adapted to the English way of life, but they have not lost touch with their own languages or the sentence structures with which they grew up. This is evident not so much from the vocabulary they use as the way in which they pronounce words or the intonation which they give to a sentence. Anybody who has been to Liverpool, or listened to the vibrant music and poetry which has come out of that city in recent years, will know it as a place where sounds of all sorts are used in exciting patterns. However, as it is difficult to explore ideas about sounds in writing, we shall concentrate on the framework around them.

Liverpool is the headquarters of 'Scouse', that Irish-based tongue that has shaped a hundred thousand comedy routines and become known world-wide through the music of the Beatles and those that have followed in their tradition. Melvyn Bragg visited Liverpool and talked to people representing different interests and communities in the city. It seemed the best place to study the way new words come into a language. Sometimes they creep in quite stealthily at first, part of a secret language which is intended to baffle outsiders. Then, gradually, they enter the mainstream vocabulary of the language, used throughout the country and, in the case of English, throughout the world.

Standing in a ship's chandlers in Liverpool's Maritime building, the historian, **Dr. Graeme Milne**, explained to Melvyn Bragg how Liverpool came to play such an important part in this development:

Liverpool is the great success story of maritime cities in England in the eighteenth and the nineteenth centuries. It was very small at the beginning of the eighteenth century and inside a hundred and fifty years it had become the nation's second port after London. It was just a real snowball of commercial success in the course of the nineteenth century. By the end of the nineteenth century it began to feel that it should have the image of a wealthy port. People were beginning to compare it with the great city ports of the ancient world or with places like Venice and Constantinople. They built huge buildings like the Liver Building and the Cunard Building that are symbolic of the wealth of the port and the big companies operating there.

Many different languages were brought here as a result of trade. At the beginning of the nineteenth century, Liverpool already had a lot of Scandinavian and Northern European merchants, Danes, Germans, Norwegians, Swedes. Then, as the nineteenth century progressed, trade with the Mediterranean countries began to expand and there was a whole new influx of traders from the Eastern side of the Mediterranean, particularly Greeks, Turks, traders from Egypt, some from North Africa. Then, later in the nineteenth century, you have Far Eastern immigration into Liverpool. Traders from India, Hong Kong, and other parts of the Far East, brought another new linguistic wave into the port.

The different groups of people brought new situations and set up their own distinct communities which still have a visible surviving identity. The Chinese community has remained a very strong and a very physical part of Liverpool's community. The European

The Victorian terrace house in the backstreets of Liverpool which a Chinese family, arriving in the country, has taken over and turned into a laundry. The Chinese community had expanded very rapidly during this century providing for themselves by setting up restaurants, laundries and other services.

immigrants, who were assimilated in the course of the nineteenth century, have had almost a century in which they've become much less visible in the culture of the city, but there is still a significant Jewish community in Liverpool that owes its origins to Jewish merchants from Central Europe and from the Middle East. Looking at the history of Liverpool in terms of its complex peoples, you have a whole range of motives for coming to Liverpool, most of which derive originally from the wealth that's been generated by trade.

It is difficult to estimate exactly how great the impact of the slave trade was on the city. Ever since the seventeenth century English ships (such as the Liverpool vessel ironically named the *Blessing*) have been exporting metals and textiles to Africa in return for African slaves who were captured, bundled into the ships in chains and taken to the West Indies to work in the plantations. From there the ships brought back sugar to England. This appalling triangular trade did not bring a great number of Afro-Caribbean people to England, but it did mean that seamen and merchants mixed with people from those countries and it is probable that in the eighteenth and nineteenth centuries more people from Africa came to live in Liverpool than came to any other English city. Nevertheless, the shameful part which the city's merchants played in the slave trade has left its scars and still provides a focus for discussion in the modern, multicultural city today.

The Irish community is probably still the strongest of the European peoples in Liverpool, as **Dr Milne** went on to explain:

They don't owe their reason for coming to the ports to trade. Most of them didn't come as merchants, they came as refugees from starvation in the nineteenth century. However, it's a fact that Liverpool is this most incredible magnet of wealth and opportunity. That brings the Irish to Liverpool in the nineteenth century rather than going further afield, and is the

Left: A large number of people emigrating to the New World around the middle of the nineteenth century died during the voyage. Rough seas, bad air below decks and meagre rations meant that those who did survive the voyage arrived in New York more dead than alive.

Right: Conditions of those emigrating in 1927 were better and many of the Irish families travelling then prospered in their new country.

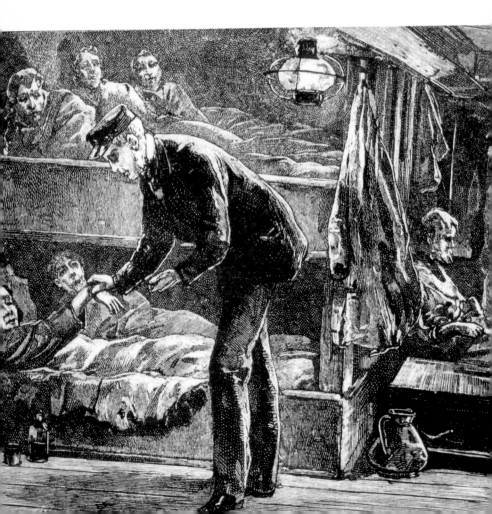

reason why so many of them came to Liverpool, planning to go to America, but ther
deciding not to do so. They stayed because Liverpool was already a great dynamic trading
city and could offer them opportunities.

Melvyn Bragg went to look at Pier Head, by the side of the Mersey, on the Liverpoo
landing stage, where the migrants from Ireland would have first set foot in Liverpool.
Many of them who came at the time of the great Irish famine in 1846 would have arrived
half starved and with no money. What they brought with them was the language o
Ireland, their love of poetry and music, their sociability and capacity for enjoyment. Those
who survived their poverty and managed to find a livelihood for themselves developed a
Liverpool dialect of their own, commonly known as 'Scouse'. Melvyn Bragg asked
Dr Gerry Knowles, who was himself born near Birkenhead just across the river, and is
now at Lancaster University, what is meant by the word Scouse. He explained where it
came from.

Scouse is the urban dialect of Liverpool, which is spoken in Liverpool itself. It's also spoken
in Birkenhead on the other side of the River Mersey, and it's spoken inland, in the western
part of Lancashire

The word itself is probably Danish and comes from a Danish dish from Lapland which is a
bit like Irish stew. I've actually seen Scouse on sale in a Danish supermarket, and the
original term is 'Labscouse.' How that has been connected with the dialect is a question
that nobody knows the answer to, but since the beginning of the century, it has come to
describe not only the language but also the people here – the 'Scousers'.

Scouse is originally a Lancashire dialect. For a long time Lancashire English was spoken here
in Liverpool, until about the middle of last century, then with the influx of lots and lots of Irish

immigrants, the language gradually changed into the Scouse as we know it now. If you listen to the intonation of Liverpool speech, in most parts of the north of England (as in England generally) at the end of the sentence the pitch will tend to go down. So, if you say to somebody "What's your name?", they'll say "John", with the pitch going down. But in Liverpool, it'll often go up - "What's your name?" "John" – it'll go up, and "What's the time?" – the pitch will go up at the end of the sentence, and that's very like some kinds of Irish English.

The way in which Irish words have come into English was discussed again in a conversation with **Professor Loreto Todd**, of the University of Leeds. Melvin Bragg asked her whether she recognised the Irish imprint on Scouse:

It is recognisable, particularly in words like 'back' where you get a type of modification of the sound at the end of the word. Those features are found in many parts of Ireland as well. Also the rhythms show it. The Irish intonation is more up and down, a bit more like the Welsh, and I can hear it in Liverpool. It's not exactly the same as any Irish one I'm familiar with, but it has certainly got a lot of overtones. Now with regard to some of the words, one of the ones I recognise very markedly as perhaps being influenced by Irish is *yous*, the plural. Also, they use *dis* and *dat* which is a feature of the south of Ireland, rather than of the north, so obviously one recognises that. Also, where I come from in Northern Ireland people tend to say *dury* products, for dairy products and it's *furries* for fairies. They say there's a *furry* at the bottom of my garden. That's very Belfast as it were. The pronunciation of *dury* and *fury* is quite similar to something that you get here as well. So, you don't only get the southern influence, as you would in *dis* and *dat* and *de Pool* for Liverpool, you get some features of the north as well. You get a type of amalgam, because it wasn't just southerners coming here, it was people from all over Ireland

IVERPOOL TO QUEBEC & MONTREAL
(ROYAL MAIL SERVICE.)

| LYNESIAN | ... | ... | ... | Thursday, Oct. 4 | SARDINIAN | ... | ... | ... | Thursday, Oct. 18 |
| RMATIAN | ... | ... | ... | Friday, Oct. 12 | PARISIAN | ... | ... | ... | Thursday, Oct. 25 |

☞ Calling at Londonderry the following day.

Of course, a lot of Irish words have come into Liverpool. It's sometimes hard to distinguish whether the word comes from Irish Gaelic or from Scots Gaelic or indeed from Welsh, because they're related languages. But I suppose the best known is *whisky*, obviously from *uisge beatha*, the 'water of life. Words like *bog* or *boggy* for something soft have come in, and possibly others, that may have had a dual etymology.

It's unique that a group of non-prestigious Irish people could have influenced a dialect so dramatically. You have the rhythms, you have the intonation, you have the passionate love of words and the love of wit. An awful lot of those Irish people arriving in the middle of the nineteenth century had nothing to live on but their wits – if they didn't use their wits they died.

Other things affected the way English was spoken in Liverpool. As a port it had a particularly interesting mix of people with different experiences. Sailors who went out from places like Liverpool came across weather conditions that they weren't used to. They picked up words like *hurricane* from the West Indies, or *tornado*, which I believe we got through Spanish. They also brought in words for food from parts of West Africa, words like *banana*, *yam*, *okra* and made them world-wide. Similarly, from the new world, they brought back *tomato* and *potato*. Of course, Liverpool was not the only port to which sailors returned with new words.

A language like *Scouse* is enriched by all the newcomers. Indian people coming here, Pakistanis coming here, people from the Caribbean in the last twenty, thirty, forty years, all bringing their overlay. The initial feeling that immigrant communities have is, first of all, they want to fit in as much as is humanly possible, so they will pick up local idioms and local traditions, and then, after they have settled, got their feet well under the table, as

Ships docking in Liverpool from all over the world
brought in the indigenous names for the products. Their
crews, likewise, used the new words they had
discovered.

were, they start wanting to express their own culture. They start bringing that in as well. And so you get accretions that will indicate different periods, different levels of influence. As a port, Liverpool is almost like a linguistic stratification. You can take a look at the various levels: the native Lancastrian, the influx of the Irish, then the influence of the black communities, the influence of the Asian communities, the Chinese communities. They all give their taste, as it were.

In another discussion, Melvyn Bragg talked to two members of the black community, Lawrence Westgaph, a native Liverpudlian whose family is from Nigeria, Trinidad, Jamaica and Ireland, and Eugene Lange, a poet. They talked about the sort of codes which particular groups of people or communities develop in order to make it difficult for outsiders to follow what they are saying. These secret languages are sometimes called *argots* – a word which was originally used to describe the sort of jargon used by thieves. Any minority group which seeks to protect its identity from the overwhelming majority culture uses code from time to time – schoolchildren, prisoners, servants and slaves, even perhaps Sloane rangers. A particular version of this is West Indian backslang in which words are pronounced as if they were spelt backwards or their pronunciation is distorted in other ways. Melvyn Bragg asked **Lawrence Westgaph** if he deliberately went out of his way to use words from the languages of other cultures:

No, not really, because the language I speak is such a part of my every day life that I'm not really conscious of the origins. I guess you realise the origins of these languages when you hear them used by people who come straight from these countries. You say 'oh wow, we say the same, we'd use that same word' in a conversation in our everyday Scouse.

Melvyn went on to ask **Lawrence** if, whilst speaking a language that belongs to him and his friends, he was proud of the fact that other people were excluded from it.

I suppose I wouldn't say I'm proud of the fact that other people don't use it, but it is a way of endearing yourself towards your friends and your family. Obviously people use language in a different way when they're speaking to people who are close to them.

Eugene Lange, a black poet from Liverpool, was asked by Melvyn why the Caribbean influence was so strong, even though many people had West African roots:

It's mainly because the black population in the UK is made up mostly of people from the Caribbean. You'll find that it's Jamaica that's got the biggest influence. From my growing up I've noticed the influence change. Say from the seventies to the eighties, it was a lot of influence from Jamaica when the Rasta Movement was going on, and now, from the mid eighties to the nineties, it's been mostly New York influence, because rap's kind of taken over and music's really the key link in what spreads the usage of different languages. People in the UK in general are influenced a lot by America and the Caribbean because they're the two big communities who have actually produced a lot of culture, an oral tradition and that's where we get our talk from mostly.

Eugene Lange: **Have you heard the expression** *whatton*? **If I say** *whatton* **browed?, it used to be** *what's going on*? **or** *what's up*?, **there's various ways of saying that.** *Whatton*?, **some people say that, and, instead of saying like** *browed*, **you might say** *dread*. **If you're a restaurant owner you'd say** *whatton dread*?. **Also Rastas used to say** *not true* **and we just say** *true* **or** *tragoo* **or** *traraboo*. **We change the word round. It's a thing called back slang. What I'm saying is 'do you know what I mean?'. Sometimes we add bits into words. I might say** *I went down taygown and bought some shamboos* – **I went down town, bought some shoes.**

116

Lawrence Westgaph added: **But the back slang isn't something that the younger generation uses as much now. It's something that's more associated with my mother's generation and maybe the generation before that. It was a way of conveying a message without having the children know what you were talking about. That was the way it was used. When I was a child, if my mother and my grandmother were talking, they'd talk like that so that the children in the house couldn't really get onto it, or couldn't really understand. So, it's not something that we use nowadays as a way of conveying a message**

On another occasion Melvyn Bragg went to St. John's market, which is a large street market selling all sorts of things from food to fur coats. A generation or two ago Jewish traders would also have been selling and shouting their wares here at St John's Market, selling fabrics and clothing mostly. These traders were often second generation immigrants and may not have spoken as much Yiddish as their parents, but, relishing their identity as Jewish market traders, they did speak a slang encompassing Yiddish, as well as Cockney rhyming, underworld, and American slang. It's known as 'Wej Patter' – 'Wej' is Jew spelled backwards. At the market, **Eddie Conway** described some of the Wej patter which he picked up as a young man while working as a market trader selling textiles:

Words like *clobber* for clothes or strides for trousers were originally market words which are now familiar to most people and widely used, but there were also specific words like *nish* for tie. That's rhyming slang, because it was from a Hebrew prayer which begins 'Nish mas col hi', so the Jewish market traders would call a tie a *nish*, which is rhyming slang and nobody else would know what they were talking about . You'd sell *gear*, you'd sell *clobber*, you'd sell *macaroni*, which is shoddy stuff – *macaroni* rhymes with *pony* – pony and trap's

crap. So there you have rhyming on rhyming. I'll give you another one: *bottle* is used, as you know, for all sorts of things, like a person's got *bottle*, he's got guts, he's got class, but if somebody's got a nice *aris* – it was usually a woman with a nice *bottle* – *Aristotle, bottle.* So you'd say – excuse the sexism here – 'this woman's got a nice *aris*', and in that way you use slang upon slang. It got very convoluted, but as long as you understood the code, you could get away with the rhyming slang. And, of course, the Yiddish speakers would understand the Yiddish part of it. It wasn't just confined to Jews, there were other people on the markets who picked this sort of language up. Originally it was an argot used by the sharp working classes in the East End of London. It originated in Petticoat Lane, but it came to be used as a 'grafters' slang' in markets all over the country and I think it was just added to, like all languages, as things changed.

All this language comes from the same sort of situations. A lot comes from the Yiddish which Jewish refugees brought with them to England. Or it comes from the underworld, and the demi-world. *In shtook*– in trouble. *Shtoom* – be quiet. *It's kosher* – it's legitimate. The term we used for being in prison was *in haida* – *haida* was the Hebrew class that you all had to go to which you didn't like. There are loads of words I could use – *dickie dirt* for a shirt, *daisy roots* for the shoes, a *barnet fair* for your hair. Another word I'm reminded of is *spieler.* – you can *spiel* on the market, you can patter on the market, or you can play cards. And the East End clubs, the non-licensed clubs, were called *spielers.* And it's also used in American back slang by the way – *spiel* comes from the Yiddish. As does *shamus* for a private eye – because that was a person who looked after a synagogue. They've all come into the English language.

Some words are used in a way very similar to the use of the word *wicked* in Afro-Caribbean

– *wicked* is *reem* and written in the paper. In Yiddish *meerskite* means ugliness, and if somebody was ugly, they'd say *the meers*'. But if something was wonderful they'd reverse *meer* into *reem*. So everything was *reem* you know – *I've got a reem whistle on* – I've got a nice suit on. So *reem* became this sort of ubiquitous word to mean good, so if you don't mind the sexism, you say 'Oh this geezer pulled a *reem kife*' – it means this fellow pulled a nice looking woman. Certain words lend themselves to back slang. Back slang, it's used quite a lot in Liverpool, – I can tell you that now.

I've got a feeling it's disappearing now, though, because the social, political, and economic situation of Jews in this country's moved on, and it's only an old rump of what we would call working class people, or people working on the markets. It may be because young Jewish people no longer have to work on the markets. If you look around, you now see first and second generation people from Pakistan or India doing exactly what these people were doing. It has always been a way out of the factories. You have to remember that, for the working class Jews, the economic alternatives were very small. What was the way out if you didn't have an education? The way out was to get on the markets and earn a few bob. And many people have done that and, of course, they developed a business from being market

e people think that Liverpool has possibly the oldest
atown in Europe. Shipping companies from
pool employed Chinese sailors and some of them,
 they got to Liverpool, decided to stay rather than
ack to sea. Most came from the south of China and
e Cantonese. This picture shows stately silk-clad
 hants in Liverpool, standing beside counters and
es which were often gilded and elaborately carved
aditional Chinese style.

raders. That situation does not arise now – in other words, young children coming from that
background are not pushed into the markets, they go into the professions. It's a sign of the
changing nature of the economic structure of the Jewish community.

Melvyn Bragg also talked to **Jatinder Verma**, Artistic Director of the London based Tara
Arts who was born to an Asian family in Tanzania and migrated to Britain in 1968. His
work has explored *Binglish* which he describes as a quirky black (British) English. He
was asked if it is important to recognise and celebrate the origins of words which have
come into the language from other cultures:

In some cases it is important, but usually it doesn't really matter because it's the very
nature of trade. One of the things that happens with trade is that goods, as they get
exchanged, change their value and often change their shape and form as well. The same
happens with words and what we should be more concerned about is how a language
expands. Certainly one of the fantastic things about English is the ways in which, over the
past few centuries, it has expanded as a result of trading and other encounters with all sorts
of other cultures. One wonderful example is the word *shampoo*, you know, we all use it now
and its origin is the action called *champa*. An English traveller first came across this
peculiar activity in the seventeenth century in South India. He describes the action of a fair
woman massaging and lathering her horse and that activity was called *champa* and from
that really comes the word *shampoo*, the thing that we all use all the time. It's not terribly
important for us when we are in our bath and are using shampoo to be aware of the fact
that this word comes from India, but it is fun to see how language expands.

One of the things that all migrants of whatever type come across is the notion of trying to
become part of the larger community, and that's always a fraught thing. On the one hand,

there's the attempt to be the same as others and, on the other is the wanting to be different. In my own experience there is this constant tussle of being English but not being only English. I began to realise that what I and a lot of my compatriots speak is more properly described as *Binglish* than English. We are quite willing to bring in other words that have some sense and meaning within our own cultures, which then, through constant use, become part of a wider culture.

One example that is really interesting to me is the word *curry*. The first time I came across it in the English context I translated it back in terms of our own food. In our food there's one particular dish called *curry*, and that's just one dish. It is not the generic word for the whole range of Indian cooking. It took me a while to realise that, in fact, I've got to drop the word *curry* as the name for a particular dish and use it now to describe anything that I eat.

But there are certain sounds which cannot be transferred. The *rr* sound in the word curry is a sort of reflexive *r*. It cannot be made in English, it doesn't exist. You can only pick it up in your babyhood, so if you don't have it around you in your babyhood, forget it, there is no chance for you unless you go through a very particular kind of training. Now with the loss of that sound you actually lose an entire sensibility, an entire taste, if you like, and that's what languages are about, they're about particular tastes. In my case now this other language is English and there are new tastes that have come into it, so to some extent, I can compensate for it, but I know that that sound I will never be able to recover. That sound does not belong in English and I have to deal with that in whatever way I can. But those are the kinds of things which we mustn't underestimate, in this talk about the traffic of languages.

It is always interesting to see the ways words come into English. Today, as I was coming into he studio, what was in front of me was a *juggernaut* and, in fact, the word *juggernaut* comes from this fantastic festival in Eastern India, the festival for *Jagannath*. The festival involves this huge chariot, which is pulled along on ropes by over a hundred men. It goes through the winding streets of a particular town and sometimes the rope slips out of the men's hands so the wheels go over the pilgrims and it's considered to be a blessing. These juggernauts have much the same kind of capacity, they can ride over you.

Of course, some communities have influenced the language of Liverpool, or Scouse more than others. Irish speech has a closeness to English, and loan words have come in from here. In a way Caribbean English has been able to infuse much more readily into mainstream English than Indian English has been able to do, partly because Indian English is at a very complicated stage. There are seventeen languages in India, whereas in the case of the Caribbean, it was always a case of constructing in English and finding its own kind of syntax. There was a degree of proximity to English, and, of course, a lot of English is imbued with Christian concepts which are also central to Caribbean or Irish culture, consequently there are many kind of values as well as associations, stories which are common currency. That has allowed for the greater infusion of Irish words and accents into mainstream English.

Sometimes words cease to be *Binglish* and become English. Shampoo and juggernaut are examples of that. Otherwise in the modern world we are not really trading with each other. Life is about trading, it is about exchanging ideas. The ways in which we exchange ideas is to have some degree of common currencies, and through those common currencies we expand our portfolio of language. I think, therefore, that there comes a moment where it's very, very difficult to trace it up. Who knows and who cares any more that these are words from Indian languages? It doesn't really matter because they have actually infused English with a certain distinctive sensibility.

During the time I have lived here there has been a massive contribution to British English from the Indian sub continent, from Australia, from the Caribbean and other places. All the new technologies that are around have actually increased that, even though the Internet is dominated by English. What's really interesting is that because the Internet has allowed so much access to so many different people, it's possible to read many different types of English. I'm not talking about different scripts, but I'm talking about actually bringing words into English and, you know, people are creating all sorts of languages of their own.

As we hover around the Millennium, nobody knows how radically computers, the Worldwide Web and e-mail are going to change our lives. It is clear that people all over the world will need to have access to a common language in order to use the next technology successfully, and it is fairly certain that English will become that global language. However, this could point in different directions. As more and more people in all corners of the world are struggling to learn English, will they lose the richness and flexibility of their own native languages, thereby giving English itself fewer opportunities to expand and grow? Or will the very fact that so many people share a common basic language mean that new dialects, new forms of expression and newly thought up words keep that language always on the move? Already the words of technology are filtering through to be used in other everyday situations. We are beginning to talk about *logging* on to a great variety of things. We talk casually about *navigators* and *web sites*, *downloading* and *formatting*. Even words like *menu, paste* and *tool* have taken on new shades of meaning.

This may be a passing fashion, but language has always been subject to fashion and fashion does not stand still. When we have used particular phrases and words for a time we drop them and take up others, shifting meanings a little each time we do it to express new attitudes and trends. Liverpool as a city has perhaps always been hospitable to new fashions and ideas and creative in adapting them, as we know from the music, poetry and other arts which have flourished here during the last fifty years. Although fewer people may be entering or leaving the port by ship, the city itself is still an exciting melting pot of ideas and cultures. The docks may be quiet, but the traffic and trade in language still clatters on.

Commissioning Editor: Angie Mason
Editor: Anne Barnes
Picture research: Caroline Jackson
Design: Graphics International
Printing: Geoff Neal Litho Ltd
CD Studs: CMCS Compact Stud™

ISBN: No 1 9017 1019

The Routes of English is presented by Melvyn Bragg
Editor:Simon Elmes
Producers: Simon Elmes and Emily Kasriel
Research: Emma-Louise Williams

CD producer: Amber Barnfather

With thanks to Broadcast Assistant Christine Saunders, Ian Gardhouse and Richard Bannerman of BBC
Features & Events.

Amongst those taking part, the production team would like particularly to thank:
Dr Kathryn Lowe, University of Glasgow,
Dr Wiliam Rollinson, Institute of Continuing Education, Liverpool
Dr April McMahon, University of Cambridge
J.C. Smith, University of Oxford
Dr Ruth Evans, University of Cardiff
Professor Frank McLynn, Strathclyde University
J. Derrick McClure, University of Aberdeen
Professors Loreto Todd and Katie Wales, University of Leeds
Dr Graeme Milne, University of Liverpool
Dr Gerry Knowles, University of Lancaster
Lisa Appignanesi
David Crystal
Arthur Dillow
John Hardacre
Ian Hislop
Mary Heslam
Terry Jones
Eugene Lange
Tommy Miller
Jatinder Verma
Lawrence Westgaph
Barbara York